ADELPHI

• 305

Humanitarian Action in War
Adam Roberts

Aid, protection and
impartiality in a policy vacuum

Oxford University Press, Great Clarendon Street, Oxford OX2 6DP
Oxford New York
Athens Auckland Bangkok Bombay
Calcutta Cape Town Dar es Salaam Delhi
Florence Hong Kong Istanbul Karachi
Kuala Lumpur Madras Madrid Melbourne
Mexico City Nairobi Paris Singapore
Taipei Tokyo Toronto
and associated companies in
Berlin Ibadan

Oxford is a trade mark of Oxford University Press

Published in the United States
by Oxford University Press Inc., New York

© The International Institute for Strategic Studies 1996

First published December 1996 by Oxford University Press for
The International Institute for Strategic Studies
23 Tavistock Street, London WC2E 7NQ

Director: Dr John Chipman
Deputy Director: Rose Gottemoeller

British Library Cataloguing in Publication Data

Data available

Library of Congress Cataloguing in Publication Data

ISBN 0-19-828093-9
ISSN 0567-932X

Contents

GLOSSARY

CERF	Central Emergency Revolving Fund (DHA)
CIA	Central Intelligence Agency
CNN	Cable News Network
DHA	Department of Humanitarian Affairs (UN)
ECHO	European Community Humanitarian Office
FAO	Food and Agriculture Organisation (UN)
FRY	Federal Republic of Yugoslavia (Serbia and Montenegro)
GONGO	Governmentally-organised non-governmental organisation
GPO	Government Printing Office (US)
IASC	Inter-Agency Standing Committee (DHA-based)
ICG	International Crisis Group
ICRC	International Committee of the Red Cross
IFOR	Implementation Force (NATO)
IFRC	International Federation of Red Cross and Red Crescent Societies
KDP	Kurdish Democratic Party
NGOs	Non-governmental organisations
ODA	Official development assistance
OECD	Organisation for Economic Cooperation and Development
ORC	Open relief centres
PKK	Kurdish Workers Party
POW	Prisoner of war
PUK	Patriotic Union of Kurdistan
RPF	Rwandan Patriotic Front
SFr	Swiss francs
UNDP	United Nations Development Programme
UNAMIR	United Nations Assistance Mission for Rwanda
UNGAR	United Nations General Assembly Resolution
UNGCI	United Nations Guards Contingent in Iraq
UNHCR	United Nations High Commissioner for Refugees
UNICEF	United Nations Children's Fund
UNITA	*União Nacional para a Independência Total de Angola*
UNITAF	Unified Task Force

UNOSOM	United Nations Operation in Somalia
UNPROFOR	United Nations Protection Force
UNRWA	United Nations Relief and Works Agency for Palestine Refugees in the Near East
UNSC	United Nations Security Council
UNSCR	United Nations Security Council Resolution
WFP	World Food Programme (UN)
WHO	World Health Organisation (UN)

INTRODUCTION

Humanitarian action as a response to war, and to violent crises within states, has been tried in the 1990s as never before. It would be easy to dismiss these efforts as failures. In Somalia, an international humanitarian involvement ended in 1995 in humiliating retreat. In Bosnia, the United Nations (UN) emphasis on humanitarian responses was mired in controversy and largely discredited by the fall of Srebrenica in 1995, which led to a significant change of Western policy. In Liberia, humanitarian agencies decided in June 1996 not to renew major operations because extensive looting resulted in their activities contributing to the war economy. The northern Iraq 'safe haven' concept was left in tatters by military actions there in September and October 1996. In Rwanda and Zaire, the record of the international community in protecting victims of genocide in 1994, and refugees in camps in 1996, has been pitiful. The litany of setbacks encompasses other conflicts, including those in the former Soviet Union.

The pendulum that swung so far towards humanitarian action in the first half of the 1990s has since then been moving in the opposite direction: such action has been in decline since a peak around 1993. Many countries are showing signs of reluctance to become deeply involved in war-torn countries and regions, even in a humanitarian role. Yet the demand for action continues. Operations are still launched, as in Zaire in November 1996. There remains an urgent need to appreciate what humanitarian action can and cannot achieve. The key issue is not whether there is a place for humanitarian action in international politics, but what that place is, and what forms such action can usefully take.

The humanitarian action that became a major part of the international community's response to the wars, civil wars and other crises of the 1990s took many forms – provision of food and shelter for refugees; airlifts of supplies to besieged populations; proclamations of 'safe areas'; attempts to ensure implementation of the laws of war; monitoring of detention conditions; the use of outside armed forces for 'humanitarian intervention' in situations of chaos, warlordism, massive atrocities and tyrannical government; mine-clearance; and post-war (even sometimes intra-war) reconstruction. Non-governmental organisations (NGOs), governments, and international bodies (especially the UN) have been deeply involved in such action.

The increase in humanitarian efforts in the 1990s contained many elements of idealism, not least a hope that it was part of a larger process whereby the sovereignty of states would take second place to the human rights of citizens. Yet governmental involvement in humanitarian action owed much to political considerations that were often tinged with an element of *realpolitik*. Most states – lacking a strong interest in the civil wars raging around the world and no longer seeing them as part of a global confrontation in which they had a stake – were nervous about any deep or enduring military involvement. They were also reluctant to accept more than a token number of refugees from these conflicts. Yet in an age of global communications the public in many democratic states demanded some positive action. All this contributed to pressures for humanitarian action on a multilateral basis, and in particular for action to assist and protect people in their own country before they became refugees, as well as to assist the repatriation of those who had left. It required new forms of humanitarian action, such as establishing safe areas and protecting aid convoys, which required a significant military role.

Yet the question of defining exactly what the military role should be and how great a commitment it required proved to be difficult and controversial. There was and remains wide agreement among governments, many non-governmental aid organisations and international agencies that external armed forces can have legitimate roles in humanitarian action – for example in protecting the delivery of relief supplies, in providing security in refugee camps, and in enforcing cease-fires so that humanitarian organisations can perform their tasks. The idea that humanitarian organisations should always operate entirely independently of armed forces has had to be modified in many cases. However, there has been remarkably little serious thinking about military protection; and the record of outside military involvement supporting humanitarian action is full of instances of vacillation and retreat, poor coordination, a reluctance to make serious commitments and take serious risks, and achieving at best only temporary results.

Overall, the experience of humanitarian action in wars has raised many difficult questions and exposed controversies concerning its purposes, effects, modes of operation, and legitimate boundaries. Does such action save lives, or prolong wars? Can it stop the killing as well as the dying? Does it imply reluctant acceptance of forcible population movements? What is the role of the military in humanitarian assistance, and does that role risk dragging states into distant conflicts? Is there a right of 'humanitarian intervention' by outside armed forces? Should safety zones be created in conflict-torn areas, and if so, how should they be protected? Does participation in humanitarian assistance by peacekeeping forces blur their impartiality and expose them to danger? Do NGOs risk losing their autonomy or impartiality when they are part of a large coordinated international response? Has the increased emphasis of governments on humanitarian action been an abdication from serious policy-making?

There is a dearth of, and a need for, objective and intellectually tough case-by-case evaluations of humanitarian action tackling questions such as these. This paper, no substitute for such studies, is a contribution towards the broader reappraisal of this subject. It reflects a dissatisfaction with that intellectual tradition (of which many soldiers, policy-makers and humanitarian workers have been part) that sees humanitarian action and tough power-political or interest-based calculation as complete opposites, and seeks to show some of the numerous points of intersection between these two approaches.

The fact remains that alongside the growth of humanitarian action there has been a policy vacuum. Major powers and international organisations have lacked long-term policies addressing the substantive issues raised by the conflicts of the 1990s. This vacuum increases the demand for humanitarian responses but reduces their effectiveness.

The central argument of this paper is that a failure to develop serious policies regarding the security of humanitarian action, and of affected peoples and areas, has been the principal cause of the setbacks of humanitarian action in the 1990s. Such security issues, the inherent difficulties of which are undeniable, have been handled repeatedly in a short-term and half-hearted manner, often with elements of dishonesty and buck-passing. A particular difficulty in discussing the question of protection is that, in some legal parlance which is reflected in that of many aid organisations, 'protection' refers not to the provision of physical security, but to efforts (for example, by Red Cross personnel) to establish and maintain a special legal status for protected persons, such as civilians and prisoners of war (POWs). Constructive thinking about security is also not assisted by the tradition, in itself honourable, of associating humanitarian action with impartiality and neutrality: sometimes the provision of security may necessitate departures from these principles. The leading Western powers, which are the ones that have been principally involved in humanitarian action, have a particular obligation to develop coherent and defensible policies regarding humanitarian crises, which will not disappear just because responding to them has created difficulties.

I. THE CHANGING CONTEXT OF HUMANITARIAN ACTION

The types of disaster that led to a growth in humanitarian action since the mid-1970s are not new. War, civil war, dictatorship, earthquake, famine and refugee flows have been familiar phenomena throughout recorded history. In the past, they rarely led to large-scale international efforts such as in the early 1990s. Clearly there were some new factors at work.

The 'Complex Emergencies' of the 1990s

One necessary condition for increased attention to humanitarian issues is the existence of disasters, especially those leading to the displacement of large numbers of people. There were many such disasters in the 1970s and 1980s, and even more in the post-Cold War world. Several totally different types of disaster have been involved:

- war (often involving civil war, general collapse of state institutions, and/or massive population displacement);
- dictatorial government (especially when in a virtual state of war with part of its own population);
- massive economic disruption and unemployment; and
- natural disasters.

The practice of states cooperating in response to some types of disaster – especially natural disasters such as earthquakes, floods and famines – is of long standing, and shows that states can sometimes take humanitarian action that is of a more or less disinterested nature, and do so effectively. In addition, man-made technological disasters, such as those at Bhopal in 1984 and Chernobyl in 1986, show the need for international humanitarian assistance. In these cases, the expertise and resources required for effective counter-measures may only be available internationally.

Wars, however, present a more complex problem. They have been the main cause of most humanitarian disasters in the 1990s, including in Afghanistan, northern Iraq, Rwanda, Somalia, southern Sudan, former Yugoslavia and some of the successor states of the former Soviet Union. In these and many other wars there has been extensive humanitarian action by states, international institutions and NGOs. The belligerent forces have often been prepared to accept humanitarian assistance from outside, or at least have been vulnerable to pressure to do so.

Most post-Cold War conflicts have been civil wars; indeed, a high proportion of wars since 1945 have been internationalised civil wars.

The civil war aspect presents some especially difficult problems for international intervention of any kind, including humanitarian action. Civil wars are notoriously bitter and difficult to control. Some of the conflicts of the 1990s, including in Burundi, Liberia, Sierra Leone and former Yugoslavia, have been characterised by a pattern of assaults on defenceless civilians and an avoidance of direct combat between adversary forces. The blurring of distinctions between combatants and civilians creates special difficulties for humanitarian action.

The term 'complex emergencies' is increasingly used to describe those humanitarian disasters of the 1990s that involve internal conflict and have elicited a multi-faceted international response. As an official United States' government publication has stated:

Complex emergencies combine internal conflicts with large-scale displacements of people, mass famine, and fragile or failing economic, political, and social institutions. Some complex emergencies are exacerbated by natural disasters and severely inadequate transport networks.[1]

The use of the term 'complex emergencies' and various synonyms ('complex crises', 'complex humanitarian disasters') does usefully describe a reality of the late twentieth century, but is also open to objection. Giving a new label to old problems does not make them any easier to solve. The term fits, perhaps too easily, the ambition of some within the UN system to tackle simultaneously and in a coordinated manner different military, political and humanitarian roles – restoring peace, assisting refugees and war victims, encouraging respect for human rights and promoting socio-economic development. Whether this is really possible is doubtful. War is the violent expression of a complex set of opposing interests and aspirations. While it may be true that complicated questions rarely have simple answers, one cannot conclude that multi-faceted answers – as the term 'complex emergencies' often implies – are necessarily right.

While this concept always implies the existence of conflict, it may not be the result of war in any simple or classical sense. Dictatorial governments acting within their own territory have been another cause of humanitarian crises. Repressive action by government may occur in the aftermath of war, as in Cambodia in the late 1970s and Iraq in the 1990s, but sometimes, as in Haiti in 1991–94, it occurs in the absence of open war. When the problem is essentially one of an over-powerful government, humanitarian agencies often find it particularly difficult to

11

act within the country concerned, and the UN Security Council has frequently been unable to take action. The responses and non-responses of the international community to the crises in Cambodia during the years of the Khmer Rouge regime (1975–79) and in Myanmar (Burma) in more recent years illustrate some of the limitations and difficulties of humanitarian action in facing extreme dictatorship.

More Refugees, Less Asylum
The steady increase of refugee flows since the mid-1970s, and of the annual expenditure for this by the UN High Commissioner for Refugees (UNHCR), is shown below.

Table 1: Refugee numbers, and UNHCR expenditures, from 1975 [2]

Year	Refugees (millions)	UNHCR Expenditure (US$ millions)
1975	2.4	69.0
1977	2.8	111.4
1979	4.6	269.9
1981	8.2	474.2
1983	10.4	397.6
1985	10.5	457.8
1987	12.4	460.3
1989	14.8	570.3
1991	17.2	862.5
1993	18.2	1,307.0
1995	14.5	1,140.0

Notes   The figures for the number of refugees are for 1 January each year, and refer only to people who have crossed an international border and have been granted asylum in another state. The figures do not include Palestinians assisted by the UN Relief and Works Agency for Palestine Refugees in the Near East (UNRWA), who numbered 2.8 million in 1995.

From 1993 onwards, the refugee figures could be supplemented by an additional category, 'other persons of concern to UNHCR'. These were as follows in 1995: internally displaced people, who have fled for similar reasons as refugees but have not crossed into another country (5.4 million), certain former refugees who have returned to their own homeland (4.0m), and war-affected populations and other groups benefiting from UNHCR's protection and assistance activities (3.5m). If these are added to the 1995 figure, the total is 27.4m.[3]

Refugee flows involve core issues in national and international politics. They can affect the stability of the states of origin and of resettlement, and they can constitute a trigger, or excuse, for military intervention. As Gil Loescher wrote in a 1992 study on the implications of refugee movements for international security:

... it is no longer sufficient to discuss the subject of refugees within a narrow national context or as a strictly humanitarian problem requiring humanitarian solutions. Too often refugees are perceived as a matter for international charity organisations, and not as a political and security problem.[4]

Loescher advocated that Western governments, particularly West European states, should 'expand existing immigration programmes, guest worker agreements and migration quotas to relieve pressures on already overburdened asylum systems'.[5] This has not happened. The increase in refugee flows has coincided with a growing reluctance of states to grant asylum. In the past, many states recognised an obligation, derived from their own experiences and buttressed by international agreements, to accept refugees. Western states also had a political-strategic interest in those refugees whose presence was proof of the failures of communist systems. In the 1990s, states have not generally reacted to crises, as they often did in the past, by accepting large numbers of refugees. This fateful change in attitudes has had important consequences.

Wars and civil wars have been the main causes of increased refugee flows. The International Committee of the Red Cross (ICRC) has gone to extremes, stating that 'with the exception of displacements caused by natural or technological disasters, the prevention of population movements corresponds essentially to the prevention of armed conflict and the prevention of abuses during armed conflict'.[6] While this statement neglects the catastrophes caused by dictatorial government, it does indicate the key role of war, and the importance of preventing war if refugee flows are to be reduced. Yet there is a reluctance on the part of states to extend the formal definition of 'refugee' to encompass those fleeing from war, anarchy, destitution and famine, as distinct from persecution. There is also a tendency not to view the 'internally displaced' – those whose flight does not involve crossing international borders – as refugees entitled to asylum.

The work of UNHCR has had to adjust to changes in the character of refugee flows and the attitudes of states towards them. In accordance with its statute, UNHCR was traditionally involved mainly in assisting refugees who had left their own countries. Over the years, in response to a series of practical imperatives, UNHCR has come to concern itself substantially with internally displaced persons; and with temporary arrangements for refugees pending their return to their homes. UNHCR and other bodies are under increasing pressure to help prevent huge influxes to other countries, to try to feed and protect threatened people in or near their own countries, and to get those who have fled to return home.[7]

The hardening of attitudes towards refugee influxes has important political and military consequences. It causes feelings of guilt, especially in countries with traditionally liberal immigration policies, and strengthens the desire to take some other form of action, including financing assistance work; it also contributes to political pressure to tackle refugee issues in or near the country of origin, for example by creating safe areas and semi-permanent camps.

Large numbers of refugees kept in camps just outside their own country can help perpetuate old conflicts and even trigger new ones. They are more likely to take military action against the regime that has caused them to flee than are those who settle into the life of another society, especially if far from the conflict. Also, such concentrations of refugees may be perceived locally as a threat, particularly if there is an armed and activist political/military leadership among them, as in the cases of the Palestinian guerrilla movements in Jordan in 1970, and Interahamwe militias among the Hutu refugees in Zaire in 1994–96. All this potential for conflict has two major consequences. First, the maintenance of security in refugee camps is a serious issue with broad policy ramifications. Second, the return of refugees to their country of origin becomes a key regional and international interest, which is likely to be reflected in the terms of peace treaties and in other pressure to go home, whether or not it is safe to do so.

Attempting to tackle crises leading to human displacement at or near the source involves, or at least should involve, addressing the question of the security of vulnerable populations, whether in their own country or in emergency camps abroad. This question was not so difficult in an earlier era when most refugees settled within a foreign country and were protected by its legal and governmental system. In the crises of the 1990s there have been many *ad hoc* answers to this problem, often devised or implemented under UN auspices. Some of these answers have proved unsatisfactory.

Changes in UN Security Council Practice

In the 1990s, the increased willingness of UN Security Council (UNSC) members to agree on common approaches, at least when not excessively burdensome, contributed to bringing humanitarian action to the fore of international politics. A small but significant measure of the increased capacity for agreement on the Security Council since the end of the Cold War is the number of resolutions passed. From 1945 to 1988 the average number of resolutions passed each year was about 15, and of vetoes cast, about five. Subsequent figures are given in Table 2.

Table 2: UN Security Council resolutions passed, and vetoed, 1990–95

Year	Resolutions passed	vetoed	Subject of vetoed resolutions
1990	37	2 (US)	Panama; Israeli-occupied territories
1991	42	0	
1992	74	0	
1993	93	1 (Russia)	Peacekeeping costs in Cyprus
1994	77	1 (Russia)	Former Yugoslavia
1995	66	1 (US)	Israeli-occupied territories

Numerous Security Council resolutions since 1989 have addressed humanitarian issues arising from armed conflicts. Indeed, the word 'humanitarian' occurred with unprecedented frequency in the resolutions of 1990–95. On this basis, many actions by peacekeeping and other bodies operating under Security Council resolutions have been directly concerned with humanitarian efforts during or in the immediate aftermath of war.

One reason for the UNSC's astonishing attention to humanitarian issues is that, in a 15-member body, it is easier to reach agreement on the lowest common denominator of humanitarianism than on more partisan or risky policies. When dealing with complex conflicts and civil wars, it may be genuinely difficult to reach a decision on a definite political line, such as supporting one side or imposing a settlement by force; it is much easier to arrive at international agreement on more modest and apparently less risky action, aimed not at the use of force but rather at the alleviation of suffering combined with efforts to induce the parties to reach a settlement. Within the framework of a large multilateral institution such as the UN there is an inevitable tendency to respond to crises by operating in humanitarian mode.

Yet there is a sting in the tail of the Security Council's preoccupation with humanitarian issues. In the end, humanitarian policies often lead to deeper involvement. It is inherently difficult for major powers to proclaim humanitarian principles and policies in relation to a conflict, and then do nothing to protect the victims and/or punish their tormentors when atrocities occur. Thus an initial humanitarian involvement can lead to a more military one – a process involving awkward changes of direction. Further, it is inherently difficult to preach humanitarianism in one crisis and then not do so in the next, however unpromising the situation and however slim the interests of outside powers. These 'ratchet' effects of humanitarian policies in the Security Council have, for better or for worse, brought humanitarianism and strategy into a curious and fateful union.

There have been many remarkable innovations in the Security Council's practice in this area. New ground has been broken, and huge numbers of lives saved. However, this has been mixed with bitter experience. The UN's humanitarian approaches are frequently criticised. Initial hopes that the UN could be the central player in limiting and ending a wide range of conflicts have yielded to more modest appraisals.

Other Factors Contributing to Humanitarian Action
Other factors have contributed to the increase of humanitarian action.
- Extensive news coverage of wars and crises, especially on television, has led to strong public pressure on outside governments to act.
- There has been a hope that, regardless of political and national differences, humanitarian action could constitute a basis for united and effective responses to a wide range of crises, and could even point the way to a new order which transcends some of the limits of the system of sovereign states.
- Some peace agreements (e.g., in Mozambique and former Yugoslavia) have contained provisions to repatriate refugees and rebuild social and economic institutions – tasks which in many cases involve assistance from humanitarian organisations.

Some other factors may be involved. The very success of efforts to control the problem of international war may also have contributed to the growth of humanitarian action. Populations of secure states, who have little direct experience of war and who seem reluctant to wage war on someone else's behalf, may be particularly inclined to react to incomprehensible conflicts elsewhere by supporting impartial humanitarian efforts in the country concerned.

The increased emphasis on humanitarian action does appear to be mainly a Western phenomenon. As Minear and Weiss have observed:

The concept of humanitarianism is most fully developed in the cultures and jurisprudence of Judeo-Christian nations. Reflecting those roots, the origin and constituencies of many of the better-known humanitarian organisations are Western ... The dominant ideologies and styles of such agencies sometimes alienate non-Western countries and populations in which major disasters have occurred.[8]

In Western states, which provide the main sources of funding humanitarian action, social developments may also have played a part in its growth. As long ago as 1970, Ali Mazrui wrote:

The growth of individualism in the West has curiously enough resulted both in reduced collective responsibility within the immediate society and increased capacity to empathise with man much further away, even in other lands altogether. The western individualist would be reluctant to contribute to the support of a distant cousin who finds himself in dire financial difficulties; and yet that same western individualist would be capable of rising to the occasion when news of a natural catastrophe in Pakistan or Chile reached him.[9]

Humanitarian Budgets
The activities and budgets of the international agencies and NGOs concerned with humanitarian action in situations of war and internal conflict reached an unprecedentedly high level in the early 1990s. In many cases there was a peak in 1993, followed by a slight decline. The overall budget of UNHCR reached US $1,307m in 1993, dropping to $1,166m in 1994 and $1,140m in 1995. Similarly, the overall budget of ICRC increased from under 400m Swiss francs (SFr) in each of the years 1986–88 to SFr811m in 1993; since then it has declined to SFr749m in 1994, and SFr641m in 1995. To give an idea of the overall scale of humanitarian action at its height in 1993–94, a very rough indication of a few of the major international agencies' expenditures on emergency relief and rehabilitation is given in Table 3.

Table 3: Expenditure of selected humanitarian agencies in 1993–94[10]

Organisation/Agency	Approx. expenditure for 1993 or 1994 (US$m)
Office of UNHCR	1,307
World Food Programme (WFP) – the food aid arm of the UN	1,200
European Community Humanitarian Office (ECHO)	900
International Committee of the Red Cross (ICRC)	519
International Federation of Red Cross and Red Crescent Societies (IFRC)	273
United Nations Children's Fund (UNICEF)	138
Oxfam UK and Ireland	115
UN Department of Humanitarian Affairs (DHA)	72

The overall global funding of emergency humanitarian assistance in 1994 has been estimated at US$7,200m, of which $1,200m came from private contributions. Virtually all the rest came from the Organisation for Economic Cooperation and Development (OECD) governments, as follows: US $1,700m, European Community Humanitarian Office (ECHO) $900m; all other OECD governments $3,400m – the nine largest donors (in order of the size of their contributions) being Germany, Sweden, the Netherlands, the UK, Canada, Norway, Austria, France and Italy. In 1995, the figures may have levelled off or even declined, suggesting an element of 'donor fatigue'.[11]

Governments have channelled a large proportion of their contributions to humanitarian assistance through international agencies such as UNHCR, as well as significant amounts through NGOs. Oxfam UK and Ireland is a case in point: of its overall budget of £103m (its highest ever) in 1994–95, £15m came from the UK government and £7m from the European Commission.[12] In yet other cases, governments have practically created NGOs (sometimes called GONGOs, or governmentally organised NGOs) to assist in one or another humanitarian project. For the most part, the tendency to act through non-governmental bodies reflects a respect for their expertise – a recognition that humanitarian assistance does properly have a large element of international and people-to-people contact – and perhaps also an anxiety not to attach the donor government's reputation too directly to actions which may go terribly wrong.

II. HUMANITARIAN INTERVENTION

Whether or not humanitarian intervention is a legal right has been discussed for centuries by international lawyers. This issue has been revived in the 1990s in international diplomacy but with some new and unexpected elements. It has become a central issue in contemporary debates on the role of humanitarian action in international relations. American writers, often keen to see the old-fashioned and reprehensible international system transformed, have seen the UN-based interventionism of the 1990s as potentially creating part of a new international order.[1] British writers have generally been more cautious.[2]

'Humanitarian intervention', in its classical sense, may be defined as military intervention in a state without the approval of its authorities, and with the purpose of preventing widespread suffering or death among the inhabitants.[3] Confusingly, the term has come to be used with a much broader and less precise meaning – major humanitarian action in an emergency situation, not necessarily involving use of armed force, and not necessarily against the will of the government. Some writers have used it in both senses.[4] The following discussion sticks to the first, classical, meaning of the term. Both of these concepts of 'humanitarian intervention' overlap with, but are not identical to, that of 'safety zones', which have been established in many different forms in conflicts of the 1990s, and are discussed further in Chapter III of this study.

Humanitarian Intervention versus Non-intervention

The idea of humanitarian intervention in its classical sense involves a violation, albeit in exceptional circumstances, of the principle of non-intervention. This rule – the prohibition of military incursions into states without the consent of the government – is often criticised as a principle based more on order than on justice, but it does have a serious moral basis. It provides clear guidelines for limiting the uses of armed force and reducing the risk of war between armies of different states. It involves respect for different societies with varying religions, cultures, economic systems and political arrangements. It acts as a brake on the crusading, territorial and imperial ambitions of states.

The actual observance of this rule has been imperfect. States have circumvented or violated it on many occasions and for many reasons, including the protection of nationals, support for opposition groups, the prevention of shifts in the balance of power and counter-intervention in response to another state which is deemed to have intervened first. Yet the principle survives, evidence, perhaps, that a robust rule can outlive its occasional violation. It has not served badly as an ordering mechanism of international relations in the post-1945 era.

Because non-intervention is such an important principle, it is not surprising that the idea of 'humanitarian intervention' has never been formally accepted in any general legal instrument. Yet even the stoutest defender of non-intervention must concede a weakness. Can that rule really apply when the situation is so serious that the moral conscience of mankind is affronted? What is the ethical or logical foundation of the rule that makes it so rigid, so uncomprehending of misery, that it cannot allow for exceptions? One might even say that if a coherent philosophy of humanitarian intervention were developed, it could have the potential to save the non-intervention rule from its own logical absurdities and occasional inhumanities.

The sheer force of circumstance which brought about the new practice, and doctrine, of humanitarian intervention can not be disputed. The age-old problem of whether forcible military intervention in another state to protect the lives of its inhabitants can ever be justified became politically sensitive when harrowing situations, extensively reported on television, led to calls for action, and when the UN Security Council, no longer hamstrung by East–West disagreement, was able to reach authoritative decisions, giving a degree of legitimacy to interventions which might otherwise have been hotly contested. Also, the dangers experienced by many humanitarian workers in the field have led to strong calls for intervention. As two leading NGOs have stated:

> The principle of sovereignty should not block the protection of the basic rights of women, men and children (including the right to emergency relief and safety) which we believe all governments are obliged to protect through the UN.[5]

Developing a coherent notion of humanitarian intervention involves questions about authorisation. The possibility that the society of states, acting through regional or global bodies, might in some way authorise particular acts of intervention significantly weakens the traditional objection to humanitarian intervention. A main foundation of the non-intervention rule has been a concern about states acting unilaterally, pursuing their own interests, dominating other societies and getting into clashes and wars with each other. If an intervention is authorised by an international body and has specific stated purposes, this concern begins to dissolve. Hedley Bull noted in 1984 that an era characterised by increased attention to human rights and focus on the UN was bound to see doctrines of humanitarian intervention revived.

Ultimately, we have a rule of non-intervention because unilateral intervention threatens the harmony and concord of the society of sovereign states. If, however, an intervention itself expresses the collective will of the society of states, it may be carried out without bringing that harmony and concord into jeopardy.[6]

Since the Second World War there has been a strong tendency for military interventions to be conducted on a multilateral basis, or at least with multilateral fig-leaves, hence the frequent use of regional organisations to sanctify such interventions as those of the Soviet Union in Czechoslovakia, of Syria in Lebanon, or of the United States in Grenada. In these and other cases 'humanitarian intervention' was often part of the justification made by those intervening.

Security Council Decisions Since 1991
Since the end of the Cold War, the UN Security Council has emerged as the main body authorising interventions, including those on humanitarian grounds, and for enunciating their purposes. In this matter the UN has obvious advantages over bodies with more limited membership. If the UN Security Council authorises an intervention, the risks of competitive chaos and insecurity and of pursuit of unilateral advantage may be greatly reduced.

The role of the UN, especially the Security Council, has given a degree of international legitimacy to uses of force that might otherwise have been open to extensive criticism. Resolutions regarding former Yugoslavia, Somalia, Rwanda and Haiti have all put great emphasis on humanitarian issues as justifications for the use of outside forces.

However, none of these five cases was a purely humanitarian intervention. The principal departure from the textbook definition was over the question of consent of the state in which the intervention takes place. In theory the absence of consent is virtually a defining feature of humanitarian intervention. In all these cases in which the UN Security Council used humanitarian justification for military involvement, the whole question of consent proved to be far more subtle in fact than it ever was in legal theory.

In northern Iraq, the UN required, in the Delphic terms of Resolution 688 of 5 April 1991, that 'Iraq allow immediate access by international humanitarian organisations to all those in need of assistance in all parts

21

of Iraq', which was less than a formal authorisation of intervention, but was nevertheless of considerable help to the US and its coalition partners. The military operation within northern Iraq which began on 17 April 1991 must be seen partly in the special context of post-war actions by victors in the territory of defeated adversaries. Further, there was Iraqi consent to the subsequent presence of the UN Guards Contingent in Iraq.

In former Yugoslavia, the Security Council resolution authorising the UN Protection Force (UNPROFOR)'s initial deployment in February 1992 was phrased to suggest that, although there was consent on that occasion, the Council might actually require the parties involved to accept the continued presence of peacekeeping forces with a humanitarian role whether they wanted them or not.[7] Subsequent resolutions on Bosnia-Herzegovina suggested that if UNPROFOR and its humanitarian activities were obstructed, further measures not based on the consent of the parties might be taken to ensure delivery of humanitarian assistance.[8] However, UNPROFOR operated for the most part on the basis of consent. Thus, although its actions in Bosnia were a clear case of humanitarian action in war, they were not a clear case of humanitarian intervention.

In Somalia, the US-led invasion of 9 December 1992 had the full blessing of UN Resolution 794 – the first to authorise explicitly a massive military intervention by member-states within a country without an invitation from the government. However, there was no Somali government to give or refuse consent, so the intervention by the Unified Task Force (UNITAF) in December 1992, and its continuation by the United Nations Operation in Somalia (UNOSOM II) in May 1993, was hardly a classic case of humanitarian intervention. Further, its actual conduct raised questions about the label 'humanitarian intervention'.

With regard to Rwanda, the initial deployment of the UN Assistance Mission for Rwanda (UNAMIR) in November 1993 was by consent of both the government of Rwanda and the Rwandan Patriotic Front (RPF). However, subsequent revisions of UNAMIR's mandate, in a series of Security Council resolutions from April 1994, gave it additional roles. Although Rwanda was a member of the UN Security Council from 1 January 1994, these new roles were not based explicitly on the consent of the government, because it was the government of Rwanda that was instigating or tolerating the mass killings. Resolution 918 of 17 May 1994 expressed concern over 'a humanitarian crisis of enormous proportions' and decided to expand UNAMIR's mandate – to contribute to the security and protection of displaced persons, refugees and civilians at risk in Rwanda, including establishing and maintaining, where feasible, secure humanitarian areas; another clause calls for providing security and support for the distribution of relief supplies and humanitarian relief operations.

This mandate was repeated and reaffirmed in Resolution 925 of 8 June 1994, which referred to 'reports indicating that acts of genocide have occurred in Rwanda', and underscored that 'the internal displacement of some 1.5 million Rwandans facing starvation and disease and the massive exodus of refugees to neighbouring countries constitute a humanitarian crisis of enormous proportions'. Great difficulties arose in gathering forces to carry out the mandate. In a further decision, Resolution 929 of 22 June 1994, the Security Council accepted an offer from France and other member-states to establish a temporary operation there under French command and control. The Council stated that in doing so it was acting under Chapter VII of the UN Charter, and it authorised France to use 'all necessary means to achieve the humanitarian objectives' set out in Resolution 925 (and also in Resolution 918 as mentioned above). This was the prelude to the French-led *Opération Turquoise* in western Rwanda in summer 1994.

There was much controversy about the French action, as indeed there was about the entire UN role, based mainly on the view that there should have been earlier, larger and more decisive humanitarian intervention. In particular, it is charged that in April 1994 no option for handling the war against civilians was presented promptly to the Security Council, which persisted for too long in seeing the problem in the familiar terms of implementing a cease-fire. Such criticisms were directed mainly at UN Security Council Resolution (UNSCR) 912 of 21 April 1994, in which, at the height of the crisis within Rwanda, the Council had actually decided to reduce the size of UNAMIR from 1,700 to 270 personnel – a decision that was never fully implemented.[9]

The crisis in Haiti following the September 1991 *coup d'état* which toppled President Jean-Bertrand Aristide led to numerous UN Security Council resolutions imposing economic sanctions and expressing concern about the humanitarian situation. The General Assembly, too, expressed its concern, for example in its Resolution 47/20 of 22 March 1993, which urged members 'to increase their humanitarian assistance to the Haitian people'. Abortive attempts to secure a negotiated transfer of power led to the passing of UNSCR 940 on 31 July 1994 authorising the use of 'all necessary means to facilitate the departure from Haiti of the military leadership ... and to establish and maintain a secure and stable environment'. This resolution is remarkable for its unequivocal call for action to topple an existing regime. It did so partly on the basis of humanitarian considerations. Following this, a US-led force intervened in Haiti in September 1994, but only after a last-minute agreement providing a basis for a US military role in Haiti, signed in Port-au-Prince by former US President Jimmy Carter and Haiti's military-installed President, Emile Jonassaint. Thus even in this case, where the UN Security Council was operating in enforcement mode, there was some hesitation in using force: some element of consent from the government in place was sought and obtained.

Questions About Consistency of UN Decisions
While none of the five cases outlined above was purely textbook, all contained some elements of humanitarian intervention. The situation in Rwanda perhaps corresponded most closely to the picture of an utterly oppressive regime slaughtering its own people. Yet the actual intervention that followed was even more hesitant and equivocal than in the other cases. All of these uses of armed force with a humanitarian rationale raise questions about the consistency and seriousness of UN practice.

The first question has to do with the terms of the UN Charter. There is the general concern that humanitarian intervention is obviously in conflict with Article 2(1): 'The Organisation is based on the principle of the sovereign equality of all its members'. There is also a more specific concern. It is sometimes suggested that the Security Council is a structurally flawed body on matters of humanitarian intervention, because under the Charter and its own past practices it cannot authorise a military action purely on the grounds of grave human-rights violations. In order to act under Chapter VII of the Charter, as it did in each of these cases, the Security Council's action must be premised on a formal determination of the existence of a threat to international peace and security. The contrast between the legal and the real grounds of action is clearest in Resolution 794 of 3 December 1992 on Somalia. It mentions 'a threat to international peace and security' once, as if to clear a necessary legal hurdle; however, the word 'humanitarian' is mentioned no less than 18 times – a dismal record for a UN Security Council resolution, but an indication of the reasoning and intentions behind the authorisation to intervene. Once a consensus has emerged that action is warranted (whether on humanitarian or other grounds), this requirement has not proved a major obstacle, but many states have been uneasy about an emerging UN practice that might one day threaten their own sovereignty.

In cases of genocide there is another possible basis for Security Council action. The 1948 Genocide Convention, Article VIII, specifies that any contracting state 'may call upon the competent organs of the United Nations to take such action under the Charter of the United Nations as they consider appropriate for the prevention and suppression of acts of genocide'.[10]

Another basis for doubt about UN practice in the 1990s has to do with selectivity and so-called 'double standards'. Undoubtedly, the conscience of mankind was shocked by the plight of Iraqi Kurds, the vicious fighting and sieges in former Yugoslavia, the starvation in Somalia and the genocide in Rwanda, but there have been other perhaps equally shocking situations in the past few decades. That genocide in Cambodia, mass shootings in Beijing, ruthless dictatorship in Myanmar or catastrophe in Sudan did not lead to humanitarian interventions suggests that other factors are involved. Such intervention seems for the most part to be confined to cases of which there has been extensive television coverage or some particular interest in intervention, and which is not likely to provoke dissent by a great power or massive military opposition. In short, it may largely be confined to highly publicised situations of war, chaos and disintegration – Somalia and Yugoslavia being prime examples – or to interventions in small states not capable of offering serious military opposition, such as Haiti. It is not an answer to the often more serious problem of the over-powerful and brutal state. True, the operation in northern Iraq in 1991 was an intervention in a state with an all-too-powerful government, but that was an exceptional circumstance: it had recently been defeated in war, and the victors felt an unusually high degree of responsibility for the plight of the inhabitants, because of US encouragement to engage in an ill-starred and brutally suppressed rebellion.

Overall, the practice of the Security Council does suggest a high degree of selectivity about situations in which humanitarian intervention might be authorised, and this selectivity involves many factors other than the plight of the people whom an intervention might be intended to assist. This parallels the Security Council's familiar selectivity in certain other spheres, such as in the question of which invaded states it assists with forceful measures. The same unheroic defence can be made of Security Council practice in both cases – prudence is not a bad guide to action, some degree of selectivity is inevitable, and it is better to uphold basic principles selectively than not at all.

A third problem with this UN practice is that it is extremely hard to divine anything like a doctrine from such a varied set of cases and approaches. Security Council resolutions have moved the matter forward inch by inch, in a thoroughly pragmatic way. The authorising resolutions offer no general defence of humanitarian intervention. Rather, they are dotted with references to the wholly exceptional circumstances of the particular case at hand. Thus UNSCR 794 of 3 December 1992 authorising *Operation Restore Hope* in Somalia contains the following wording in the preamble at the express wish of African states: 'Recognising the unique character of the present situation in Somalia and mindful of its deteriorating, complex and extraordinary nature, requiring an immediate and exceptional response'. In other words, they did not want the invasion of Somalia to be viewed as a precedent for invasions of other sovereign states.

This reluctance to define a doctrine of 'humanitarian intervention' may stem from a sense that to give explicit legal approval to the principle may be to open a door that is better kept closed. If the door must sometimes be opened, there should be an awareness before passing through it that the other side is legally questionable territory.

Purposes and Results of 'Humanitarian Interventions'
The greatest difficulties arising from this contemporary practice of interventions with a humanitarian rationale have to do with their uncertainty of purpose, their inadequate means, and their questionable consequences. In interventions, what does the word 'humanitarian' mean, and does it accurately describe anything beyond the original motive? How can this translate into actual policies to transform a situation? Does it make sense to call an intervention 'humanitarian' when the troops involved may have to fight and kill those who, for whatever reasons, seek to obstruct them? Or when the troops involved fail to provide what the inhabitants most desperately need – including security?

In many instances of 'humanitarian intervention' since 1990, the repeated emphasis on the word 'humanitarian' has gone hand-in-hand with the absence of a serious long-term policy with respect to the target country, except in the limited matters of providing food and medical aid, and trying to get rival factions to reach a peace accord. Some of the emphasis on humanitarianism is vulnerable to the criticism that it reflects the natural desire to do *something* in the face of disaster, and a tendency to forget that in all these cases the disaster has been man-made, and requires changes in policies, institutions and possibly even in the structure of states and their boundaries.

The vagueness and incompleteness of the aims in some of these interventions is striking. In northern Iraq, the extent to which Kurdish autonomy was or was not supported was unclear. In former Yugoslavia, the mandates of UNPROFOR varied from place to place and from time to time, but were widely viewed by the inhabitants as inadequate. In Somalia, the mandates of the forces intervening under UN auspices were never clear on the key issues of who was in charge of the country's administration, and what was to be done about the weapons and warfare of the clans and warlords. In Rwanda, many critics have asserted that the UN should have had a more forceful policy, and should perhaps have sided with the RPF forces. In all these cases, there are reasons for the vagueness of goals: more precision would have implied a willingness to impose a pre-determined outcome, would have been open to the accusation of dictatorial interference, and would in any case probably have split the Security Council.

The results of the post-1990 cases of intervention have been, at best, mixed. In northern Iraq, there was a temporary improvement in the situation in the Kurdish areas; yet even there, the modest security that was achieved for the Kurds in 1991 remained under constant threat. The original intervening forces, led by the US, were not willing to stay, nor to stop the strife between different Kurdish factions which always threatened to drag in the neighbouring powers of Turkey, Iran and of course, Iraq. The US Central Intelligence Agency (CIA)'s efforts to influence political developments in the area, far from offering protection, made the Kurdish individuals involved vulnerable to reprisals in September 1996 when Iraqi forces re-entered some cities in the Kurdish region.

In the absence of a clear policy and a strong governmental force in the area, the original US-led intervention proved to be a step onto a slippery slope, helping to create the conditions for further interventions. From August 1991, Turkish forces launched attacks in northern Iraq against their foes in the Kurdish Workers Party (PKK); a Turkish military operation in March 1995 was particularly extensive, involving some 35,000 troops; and in 1996 there were further major Turkish military campaigns against PKK bases in northern Iraq. Iranian forces actively supported the Patriotic Union of Kurdistan (PUK). Throughout, there was much nervousness about whether Saddam Hussein's government and armed forces could be kept indefinitely from re-entering the region and wreaking vengeance on their adversaries, which is what eventually happened by invitation from the Kurdish Democratic Party (KDP) in September 1996. Many lives were saved by establishing the 'safe haven', especially in 1991. Inasmuch as the 'safe haven' has continued in some form, it is because it reflects not only a humanitarian involvement, but also a US strategic interest in keeping Iraq down. It constitutes a warning of what can go wrong with humanitarian intervention.

In former Yugoslavia, UNPROFOR did fulfil some humanitarian purposes. It assisted with the delivery of food and other supplies to Sarajevo. However, both in Bosnia and in the Serb-held areas of Croatia, it failed conspicuously to protect the inhabitants from their adversaries. To the modest extent that UN involvement in Yugoslavia can be considered a case of humanitarian intervention, it is one which exposes certain limitations to the idea, at least when there is no real willingness to provide protection.

In Somalia, the follow-up to *Operation Restore Hope* of December 1992 was sadly reminiscent of colonial policing. The words of the UN military spokesman in Mogadishu on 10 September 1993, the day after yet another incident in which UN troops killed a number of civilians, are an appropriate epitaph for short-sighted optimism. 'Everyone on the ground in that vicinity was a combatant, because they meant to do us harm'. The UNOSOM II peacekeeping operation left the country in March 1995 having saved many who would otherwise have starved, but without having achieved a major change in the chaotic clan warfare that had led to the UN's initial involvement in 1992.

In Rwanda, despite ample early warning, the interventions under UN auspices within the country were limited in size, in duration and in goals. This sad experience illustrates the reluctance of states to take decisive and enduring action in a situation of great danger, especially where they have few direct interests.

The operation in Haiti had an unusually clear stated purpose – the restoration of a democratically elected government. There was also a strong motive for intervention as a means of stopping refugee flows to neighbouring states, including the US. Here intervention seems to have been successful, partly because the US was committed to change. However, any optimism must be tempered by awareness of the very limited long-term results of previous US interventions: huge difficulties were encountered earlier in the twentieth century when trying to eradicate violence and dictatorship from Haitian politics.

The results of international intervention in internal conflicts since 1991 have been, at best, mixed. As Lori Fisler Damrosch has written, 'In the eyes of many, collective institutions have done little to restrain internal conflicts: rather, it is the institutions themselves that seem under restraint'.[11]

Problems with the 'Humanitarian Intervention' Concept

The 1990s practice of humanitarian intervention has resulted from real and urgent crises. It has also introduced innovative features, the most significant of which is the emphasis on the UN Security Council as the authorising body, and it has undoubtedly saved many lives. However, five serious problems have been exposed.

- The term 'humanitarian intervention' is a misnomer, a justification which should be viewed sceptically. It carries the implication that military intervention in another country can be humanitarian in four respects – in its original motives, in its stated purposes, in its methods of operation and in its actual results. There are doubts as to whether such action can really be humanitarian in any, let alone all, of these ways. In particular, an intervention force in a crisis-torn country, in order to bring an end to the conflict that caused its dispatch there, may need to take tough action, or even to take sides, in ways that go well beyond the normal meaning of 'humanitarian intervention'.

- The claim that an intervention by one's own forces is 'humanitarian' – the provision of assistance to unfortunate peoples incapable of providing for themselves – appeals too easily to ethnocentric tendencies. An operation armed with moral rectitude but potentially weakened by contempt for local forces can easily degenerate into arrogance, anger, bathos and despair.

- Any intervention is liable, sooner or later, to provoke local opposition. Even humanitarian assistance can rouse strong local resentment, especially if the very necessity for its presence cruelly exposes failings in the target society, or if the forces involved are substantially ignorant of, or arrogant towards, local forces and customs with which they have no long-term relationship. Thus what begins as humanitarian intervention risks ending in humiliating exit.

- A multilateral intervention, authorised by the Security Council, is especially at risk due to certain inevitable features of the way the UN goes about its collective business – compromise, inertia, formal impartiality and (sometimes) avoidance of difficult issues. There may be a lack of clear strategic direction in any operation, a lack of knowledge of the country and its languages, a lack of any deep commitment or sense of responsibility on the part of troop-contributing states, and a lack of willingness to take on governmental functions.

- There are structural causes for the commonly encountered tension between armed forces engaging in humanitarian intervention and the humanitarian organisations whose work they assist. Such organisations value their independence and/or impartiality. If they cooperate in armed interventions for humanitarian purposes, they may end up acting as humanitarian auxiliaries of armed forces, and perceived as accomplices in any excesses.[12]

There is absolutely no possibility of securing general agreement among states about the legitimacy of humanitarian intervention. The many interesting attempts to devise formal criteria for intervention are not likely to win the approval of more than a handful of states.[13] Humanitarian intervention will, and perhaps should, remain in a legal penumbra, as something which may occasionally be approved by the Security Council or by other bodies, may reluctantly be tolerated by states, but cannot be given any generic advance legitimation. Such legitimation is unattainable not only because intervention involves breaking a valued norm, but also because it is impossible to spell out in advance the circumstances in which such interventions might conceivably be justified. The fear of such action getting out of hand is not unreasonable. In too many states there are living memories of external domination, and real fears that outsiders, in the name of humanitarianism, could find more or less plausible grounds for intervention. To reopen the door to external interventions in any general way would be deeply unpopular in many states, often for very good reasons. In addition, power political calculations of several kinds necessarily enter into considerations of whether a particular intervention should be initiated or supported, and provide a further bulwark against the emergence of a doctrine of humanitarian intervention.

Despite the frequency of cases since 1991 involving strong elements of humanitarian intervention, the twin principles of sovereignty and non-intervention remain fundamentally important in the international system. These principles may be modified through a wide variety of trans-national developments and international institutions, but only in very extreme cases, and with a wide range of procedural and substantive safeguards, can they be directly overridden by overt cases of humanitarian intervention. This is one reason why, in many situations, the Security Council has in the end preferred action that is more modest than full-scale humanitarian intervention. In actual practice, it has often ended up seeking to protect inhabitants with such devices as 'safe areas' and other forms of safety zones, often with the consent of the states in which they are situated.

III. FORMS OF HUMANITARIAN ACTION

The rise of humanitarian considerations as part of the conduct of international relations in the early 1990s was by no means limited to the extreme case of 'humanitarian intervention'. Several other distinct forms of humanitarian action were implemented in the midst of ongoing wars, including the delivery of relief supplies, the use of UN peacekeeping forces for humanitarian purposes, and the establishment of safety zones. There were also attempts to develop international administrative roles, and to punish violations of the laws of war. All these approaches achieved some results, but also had problems and involved controversy. Sometimes different actions taken for different humanitarian purposes conflicted with each other.

Delivery of Humanitarian Relief During Wars

Debates about the delivery of food and other supplies to beleaguered populations during wars has a long history. Early in the First World War, the US government considered a plan for supplying food to Germany, which was badly affected by the Allied blockade. It did so partly because it was alarmed by the conduct of both the UK and Germany towards neutral shipping, and especially by a war-zone plan proposed by Germany which would have had a particularly adverse effect on US trade. The US Secretary of State reported to President Wilson, 'I am led to believe from Conversations with the German and Austrian Ambassadors that there would be a chance of securing the withdrawal of the military zone order in return for favorable action on the food question.'[1] He then went on to propose an agreement covering four points, of which the first was food:

> Food sent to Germany for the use of non-combatants, to be consigned to American agents and by American agents delivered to retail dealers licensed for that purpose by the German Government – the license specifying that the food so furnished was to be sold to non-combatants and not to be subject to requisition. Any violation of the terms of the license could work a forfeiture of the right of such dealers to receive food for this purpose.[2]

This plan was deeply resented, especially in the UK, where it was deemed a German blackmail proposition and interpreted to mean 'free food to Germans after they have done their best by mines and torpedoes to cut off England's food'.[3] It was not in the end implemented, but many other programmes were, especially in 1917–18.[4] It is, however, a useful illustration of how easily humanitarian aid can become entangled with other issues, and how assertions that food aid will benefit only non-combatants can seem unconvincing.

Although there have been many such failures, war has also been the midwife of modern humanitarianism, leading to the birth of major organisations dedicated to humanitarian relief. Many have acquired important roles in peace as well as war. What is now ICRC was founded after the Battle of Solferino in 1859. The First World War led to the creation of the Save the Children Fund in the UK and the American Relief Association in the US. Oxfam was founded in 1942 out of concern about delivering food in the Balkans. *Médecins sans Frontières* was formed in 1971 following the Biafran war. In all these cases the perception that these bodies did not represent states, especially belligerent states, was crucial to their credibility. ICRC, in particular, maintained its reputation for impartiality by avoiding partisan statements, and by maintaining confidentiality in such humanitarian activities as visits to POW and internment camps.

Delivery of humanitarian aid during war provokes awkward questions about the consequences of such action. It is often asserted that:

- A proportion of humanitarian aid ends up in the hands of belligerent forces. This can happen for many reasons. Aid may be commandeered at gunpoint, an aid agency may build a working relationship with one particular party, and even the best distribution system may not be able to prevent supplies from getting through to armed forces.

- Even if delivered solely to civilians, aid can still favour one side more than the other, for example, if the aid is delivered directly to a city which is the capital of a country at war (such as Sarajevo), or if the aid enables locally produced supplies to be directed to the armed forces.

- By propping up one or both belligerents, and postponing the onset of war-weariness, aid may actually have the perverse effect of prolonging wars, and ultimately increasing the death, destruction and suffering which they cause.

- There are frequently powerful pressures on agencies to give more aid to one side than another, or even to withhold aid altogether from some parties in the hope that this will induce them to make political compromises.

- Some humanitarian deliveries, especially if conducted by a state rather than an international organisation, may contain or be accompanied by supplies of arms.

Accusations that aid can have some of these effects were frequently made with respect to former Yugoslavia in 1991–95; it is a fact (though one which can be justified in several ways) that international aid organisations and NGOs were far more heavily involved in Bosnian government-held areas than in the Serb-held ones, and that some aid did find its way to the armies involved. Sometimes, indeed, aid may be given deliberately to assist one side in a conflict. This was the case with aid to the Cambodian refugee camps on the Thai border in the early 1980s.

In many recent wars, humanitarian organisations involved in aid delivery have had genuine difficulty asserting their autonomy and immunity. The delivery of aid has resulted in threats to the humanitarian workers involved and widespread seizure and looting of aid shipments. In Liberia in June 1996, such problems led Oxfam and 12 other humanitarian agencies, including ICRC, to decide not to renew major operations. Subsequently, the UK and US governments, and the European Union, followed a similar policy. As David Bryer, Director of Oxfam, has stated:

> The Liberian warlords had looted more than four hundred aid vehicles and millions of dollars of equipment and relief goods, and those thefts had directly supported the war, and caused civilian deaths and suffering. The vehicles and radio equipment had been used for military purposes, and sold, along with diamond and gold deposits which the different factions control, to purchase arms ... In this case, I do think that more lives are likely to be saved by preventing such looting than by providing humanitarian aid ... protection from violence is more vital than humanitarian relief ... What I don't accept is that such abuse of aid necessarily means that we should not do it. The question to ask is whether such abuse means that the *net* impact of that aid helps civilians fulfil their rights to material necessities and protection from violence. In Liberia and, looking back, in Somalia, I think the answer is on one side. In Bosnia and in Zaire, I think it is on the other, and that we have been right to stay.[5]

The concept of 'humanitarian space' has been advanced in order to invoke the idea that aid operations, even in the midst of war, should be free from interference of various kinds.[6] However, the concept remains ill-defined and ineffective. The weaknesses, evasions and ambiguities that surround it are evidence of the difficulty that some international and humanitarian organisations have in coming to terms with the critical importance of physical security, both of humanitarian operations themselves, and of the people they are supposed to assist.

Use of UN Peacekeeping Forces for Humanitarian Purposes

In the post-Cold War world, and to an unprecedented extent, forces operating under a UN mandate have become involved in a wide range of humanitarian tasks. These have taken the following main forms:

- Protecting humanitarian relief workers, such as those representing international agencies and NGOs, from attacks by belligerents and generally from the dangers of war.
- Directly engaging in humanitarian action, for example delivering humanitarian relief supplies, maintaining essential services and reconstructing damaged buildings.
- Facilitating contacts between adversaries over such matters as resettlement of refugees and visits to grave sites.
- Establishing certain designated areas ('safety zones') where a high degree of protection is intended for the inhabitants from the threat or use of force.

Such tasks were a key part of the UN's effort in several war situations, including in former Yugoslavia, Somalia and Rwanda. Peacekeeping forces have been deeply involved in such activities, sometimes as an almost complete substitution for traditional peace-keeping activities, such as manning cease-fire lines, since in these conflicts there was often little or no peace to keep. Other forces and agencies operating in association with the UN have also been involved in these various humanitarian tasks. For an international organisation such as the UN to attempt this in the midst of ongoing wars is historically unprecedented. The tasks are by nature extremely difficult, and also controversial.

This change in practice has not always been reflected in general statements about the purpose and character of peacekeeping.[7] Within the UN, against a background of multiple and difficult commitments of peacekeeping forces, humanitarian issues have not loomed large in attempts to establish criteria that should be considered before new tasks are undertaken. A UN Security Council Presidential Statement on Peacekeeping, issued on 3 May 1994, listed six factors which must be taken into account when a new operation is under consideration. These are the existence of a threat to international peace and security, whether regional bodies are ready to assist, the existence of a cease-fire, a clear political goal which can be reflected in the mandate, a precise mandate and reasonable assurances about the safety of UN personnel.[8] This list contained no reference to humanitarian operations in the midst of continuing hostilities, and indeed suggested a natural desire to return to something more like normal peacekeeping. Two days later, on 5 May 1994, the Clinton administration's long-planned Presidential Decision Directive 25, on 'multilateral peace operations', did suggest that one relevant consideration for the US when voting on a military operation proposal under UN auspices would be whether there was an 'urgent humanitarian disaster coupled with violence'. There would also have to be consideration of 'the political, economic and humanitarian consequences of inaction by the international community'.[9]

There have been some remarkable successes in using UN peacekeeping forces for humanitarian purposes in situations of war, civil war and breakdown of government. Many lives have been saved and refugee flows limited by some of these humanitarian actions. Sarajevo, where a population of well over 350,000 was at risk during the siege, is a case in point. Despite the many failures and interruptions, the maintenance of supplies – gas, water and electricity, as well as food and materiel brought in by land convoys and air – did effectively mitigate many of the extreme cruelties of siege warfare.

This achievement would have been impossible without UN peacekeeping forces. The figures for supplies brought in by the UNHCR airlift are impressive. The longest-running humanitarian air-bridge in history, it lasted from 30 June 1992 to 5 January 1996. Although there were many periods when, due to Serb threats, it was not possible for aircraft to fly to Sarajevo at all, during the three-and-a-half years of the airlift there were 12,951 sorties delivering 160,677 tonnes, of which 144,827 were food and the rest non-food items (such as shelter materials and medical supplies).[10] In other words, an average of about 125 tonnes a day was delivered. During many months of the war the airlift provided more than 85% of all assistance reaching Sarajevo. In addition, over 1,000 patients were medically evacuated by air, plus over 1,400 of their relatives.[11] While the Sarajevo airlift was remarkable in the hostile circumstances, the overall tonnage delivered in three and a half years was about the same as the average delivered each month in the Berlin airlift of 1948–49.[12]

The special problems attendant upon humanitarian efforts by

peacekeeping forces in situations of great violence have been well publicised. They fall under the following headings:

- Humanitarian action often involves compromises with belligerents, making impartiality difficult to maintain. Any action in the midst of an ongoing conflict requires consent of the parties on the ground. Convoys cannot move, aircraft cannot fly and hospitals cannot operate if there is no such consent. Thus peacekeepers inevitably find themselves dealing closely with one belligerent or another.
- Humanitarian action often favours one side more than the other, further straining the credibility of the peacekeepers' impartiality. Relief supplies are often, and for good reasons, provided more to one side than to another; so is the protection afforded by the establishment and maintenance of specially designated safety zones.
- While the peacekeepers' impartiality is often considered essential during an ongoing conflict, it is particularly hard to maintain while conducting or authorising military actions that are seen as partial to one side – such as enforcing economic sanctions and 'no-fly zones', punishing infractions of cease-fire agreements, or pressing a recalcitrant party to accept a particular approach to a settlement.
- Personnel carrying out humanitarian work in the midst of ongoing conflict usually have to be dispersed to many parts of a war zone, making them exceptionally vulnerable to reprisals and hostage-taking by belligerents. When the personnel involved are troops supplied for a peacekeeping operation, their vulnerability can inhibit powers from taking forceful military action even when this seems to be required.
- It can be very difficult to recruit and maintain troops with the necessary training and discipline to carry out peacekeeping/humanitarian tasks in a war zone, and generally to mobilise political, diplomatic and financial support in a long war if major powers do not see that their interests are directly affected.
- The heavy demands of running peacekeeping/humanitarian missions in a large number of conflicts simultaneously has exposed certain limits to the UN's capacity to manage operations, and (even more dramatically) the political and resource limits within which the UN has to operate. Many states have been unwilling to provide all the forces, materiel and finance required for such operations. Consequently there has been pressure to handle more problems on a regional basis.

These problems proved exceptionally debilitating in both Somalia and Bosnia. The sense that humanitarian issues were among the factors that made it harder to stick to tried-and-tested notions of peacekeeping was evident in UN Secretary-General Boutros Boutros-Ghali's January 1995 report, *Supplement to an Agenda for Peace*. In the passage below he seemed to hold the humanitarian cart responsible for running over the peacekeeping horse:

There are three aspects of recent mandates that, in particular, have led peace-keeping operations to forfeit the consent of the parties, to behave in a way that was perceived to be partial and/or to use force other than in self-defence. These have been the tasks of protecting humanitarian operations during continuing warfare, protecting civilian populations in designated safe areas and pressing the parties to achieve national reconciliation at a pace faster than they were ready to accept. The cases of Somalia and Bosnia and Herzegovina are instructive in this respect.[13]

Boutros-Ghali went on to indicate that 'additional mandates that required the use of force ... could not be combined with existing mandates requiring the consent of the parties, impartiality and the non-use of force. It was also not possible for them to be executed without much stronger military capabilities than had been made available'.[14] This is a classic reflection of the view, drawn largely from Somalia, that it was disastrous for UN forces to cease to be impartial and to use too much force. This is not the only possible interpretation of the causes of failure in Somalia, but it prevailed, leading many in the UN and elsewhere to be extremely cautious in Bosnia.

Events in Bosnia in 1992–95 suggested that the relationship between humanitarian and peacekeeping roles, while extraordinarily complex, can have positive aspects. Despite all the disappointments, the presence of UN peacekeeping forces, whose mission was largely to support humanitarian action, may have reduced at least slightly the incidence of extreme atrocities, helped prevent a process of creeping unilateral interventions in the war and may even have prepared the way for a peace settlement by demonstrating the readiness of the international community to assist and monitor such an outcome.

In the months leading up to the General Framework Agreement for Peace in Bosnia and Herzegovina agreed at Dayton, Ohio in November 1995, the relationship between humanitarian action and a peace settlement was especially complex and paradoxical. The Security Council repeatedly asserted that there was such a connection: 'the provision of humanitarian assistance in Bosnia and Herzegovina is an important element in the Council's effort to restore international peace and security in the area'.[15] This may in the end have been true, but with a qualification. It was not so much the attempt to provide humanitarian assistance itself, but rather the Serb rejection of that attempt in the first half of 1995, which created the conditions for the serious effort of August–November 1995 to restore peace and security in the area. A more robust policy of decisive enforcement action only became possible in Bosnia after the humanitarian aid programme had practically stopped in mid-1995 due to Bosnian Serb actions. Once UNPROFOR no longer had personnel widely spread out and hence vulnerable to Serb retaliation, it was more able to act, and once the Bosnian Serbs had shown contempt for humanitarian efforts, for the 'safe areas' and for the Security Council, there was more reason to act. Thus the Western powers, and the UNPROFOR commanders, became less cautious about authorising a major use of force by NATO, as they eventually did in *Operation Deliberate Force* in August 1995. In short, a humanitarian involvement, especially in the 'safe areas', had a 'ratchet' effect, leading eventually to a major NATO military campaign.

Safety Zones

'We don't need food. We need safety'. A placard with these words was carried by a refugee child in Safwan, in the demilitarised zone in southern Iraq, in April 1991.[16] Agencies are frequently concerned primarily about the delivery of food, blankets and medical supplies, when in many wars what is needed above all is security. Sadako Ogata, the UN High Commissioner for Refugees, has recognised the problem with admirable frankness. 'Humanitarian assistance is much more than relief and logistics. It is essentially and above all about protection – protection of victims of human rights and humanitarian violations'.[17] However, providing security frequently stretches the limits of humanitarian efforts and challenges the idea of impartiality.

One approach to the provision of security is safety zones. The idea that certain areas should enjoy special protection, even in the midst of ongoing war, has long been reflected in provisions of the laws of war. For example, the 1907 Hague Convention IV, Article 27, states:

> In sieges and bombardments all necessary steps must be taken to spare, as far as possible, buildings dedicated to religion, art, science, or charitable purposes, historic monuments, hospitals, and places where the sick and wounded are collected, provided they are not being used at the time for military purposes. It is the duty of

the besieged to indicate the presence of such buildings or places by distinctive and visible signs, which shall be notified to the enemy beforehand.

The 1949 Geneva Conventions provided for the establishment of 'hospital zones and localities', which would normally involve prior agreement between the belligerents, to protect wounded, sick and aged persons, children under 15 years of age, expectant mothers and mothers of children under seven.[18] They also provided for the establishment, by agreement between the belligerents, of 'neutralised zones' to shelter wounded and sick combatants or non-combatants, as well as civilians who take no part in hostilities.[19] The 1977 Geneva Protocol I added a provision for 'demilitarised zones' by agreement between the belligerents.[20] All these arrangements have obvious limitations. They are based on the assumptions that the security zone is a very limited area, that all combatants and mobile military equipment have been withdrawn and that no acts of hostility would be committed by the authorities or the population. They require consent, in most cases formal, between belligerents; they depend on complete demilitarisation of the area, which is hard to achieve in practice; and they do not specify arrangements for defending the areas or for deterring attacks on them.

The post-Cold War period has seen significant variations on these arrangements.[21] There have been several attempts to create areas of special protection, in which the victims of a conflict and the humanitarian bodies that assist them can have a degree of safety. Such areas have been variously called 'corridors of tranquillity', 'humanitarian corridors', 'neutral zones', 'open relief centres', 'protected areas', 'safe areas', 'safe havens', 'secure humanitarian areas', 'security corridors' and 'security zones'. The Security Council has been active in promoting such zones, and has itself used at least five of these terms for them.[22] The UNHCR has also had a significant role in promoting these concepts, and indeed itself established on the basis of consent two 'open relief centres' (ORCs) in Sri Lanka, where local inhabitants could take refuge when threatened by the conflict between government forces and Tamil rebels.[23] The variety of terminology is a reflection of the wide range that such areas can assume, and the absence of a standard legal concept.

Five features of most of the areas of special protection as actually established have been as follows:
- different nomenclature from that specified in the conventions has been used;

- areas of special protection have generally been proclaimed or supported by outside states and international bodies, especially the UN Security Council, rather than by the belligerents themselves;
- outside military forces have in all cases except Sri Lanka had responsibilities for protecting these areas;
- a central concern has been with the safety of refugees, and the prevention of massive new refugee flows; and
- military activity of one kind or another by local belligerents has sometimes continued within the areas of special protection.

The major area of special protection in the post-Cold War era, which contributed to the development of the concept elsewhere, was northern Iraq in the immediate aftermath of the 1991 Gulf War. Following a failed uprising which the Western powers helped to incite, huge numbers of people, mainly in northern and southern Iraq, fled their homes, many ending up on the Iranian and Turkish borders. Starting on 17 April 1991, a military operation by US, UK and French forces helped to establish a 'safe haven' in part of Iraq north of the 36th parallel. This was to enable some 400,000 mainly Kurdish refugees on the Turkish border to return to a degree of safety in northern Iraq. UN Secretary-General Javier Pérez de Cuéllar initially expressed doubts about this move, saying that it posed a legal problem 'even if there is no difficulty from the moral and humanitarian point of view'.[24]

On 18 April, as a result of extended negotiations with the Iraqi government, UN officials secured an agreement to allow humanitarian aid workers and relief supplies access to Iraq's entire population, including Kurds and Shi'a refugees. On 21 April, the Iraqi government requested that the UN Secretary-General assume responsibility, within the framework of the 18 April agreement, for the transit centres at Zakho in northern Iraq. Following this request, UNHCR assumed responsibility for humanitarian assistance in the coalition's security zone by mid-June 1991. This was the framework within which the coalition troops were replaced by a 500-strong United Nations Guards Contingent in Iraq (UNGCI). This contingent was drawn from the UN Guards, whose role is essentially that of doormen at UN premises, and it was given a unique status, being neither a peacekeeping force nor an enforcement body. Its formal task was to protect all staff, equipment and supplies of the Inter-Agency Humanitarian Programme in Iraq. It was presented to Baghdad as direct and limited support to the humanitarian operation, and to the Kurds (especially through a massive leaflet campaign) as a real safeguard which would allow them to return. Many

Kurds thus repatriated voluntarily, but their decision to do so was in part based on false assumptions.

With the deployment of UNGCI, the main military back-up for the 'safe haven' in northern Iraq became an external one – the ominously entitled *Operation Poised Hammer* in Turkey, by which the coalition, even after its troops had withdrawn from northern Iraq, threatened Iraq with air attack if it did not comply with the various terms imposed on it. Having been initially established without the consent of the Iraqi government, the 'safe haven' in northern Iraq was not just an unusual safety zone, but also an unorthodox case of 'humanitarian intervention'. Its special features included the fact that it was established by the forces of three or four powers with only a limited degree of authority from UN Security Council resolutions, and that there was no chance of completely disarming the area, as it was inhabited by Kurds for whom bearing arms and internecine warfare is a way of life. It has endured for five years, which is longer than any other contemporary safety zone, but the protection offered is increasingly eroded. Its central limitation – that there was neither the capacity nor the will either to stop or significantly influence local military activities – was its undoing; military forces from Turkey, Iran and eventually Iraq itself went in, or were invited in, to support factions they viewed as friendly and to fight those which they saw as a threat.

The 'safe areas' in Bosnia and Herzegovina in 1993–95 also ran into problems largely because of the inherent difficulty of controlling military activities within the safe area as well as activities against it. Established during war, with the consent of the host government, they were designed to protect the inhabitants of six towns (including large numbers of refugees who had fled to them) from Bosnian Serb forces who were in a position to besiege them, and were militarily predominant. This was bound to be a particularly difficult task.

The language of the resolutions establishing the 'safe areas' in Bosnia suggests that humanitarian considerations loomed large in the Security Council. The initial resolution of April 1993 demanding 'that all parties and others concerned treat Srebrenica and its surroundings as a safe area which should be free from any armed attack or any other hostile act' used the word 'humanitarian' eight times, including three condemnations of violations of international humanitarian law.[25] These concerns were also reflected in the resolution of May 1993 extending the concept of 'safe area' to five additional threatened areas: Sarajevo, Tuzla, Zepa, Gorazde and Bihac. This declared that the concept of 'safe area' involved 'full respect by all parties of the rights of UNPROFOR and the international humanitarian agencies to free and unimpeded access to all safe areas in the Republic of Bosnia and Herzegovina and full respect for the safety of the personnel engaged in these operations'.[26] The geographical limits of most of the safe areas were never defined.

The events in and around the 'safe areas' in 1993–95 provided poignant proof that the proclamation of humanitarian goals still leaves a host of questions to be addressed. The most difficult one was how the UN, or NATO, was going to protect these areas. A June 1993 resolution provided a dual framework for the use of force in aid of the safe areas. On the one hand, UNPROFOR was authorised to 'deter attacks against the safe areas', and also, 'acting in self-defence', to take action dealing with bombardments against, and armed incursions into, them. On the other hand, 'UN Member States, acting nationally or through regional organisations or arrangements' (a clear reference to NATO) were authorised to take, in coordination with the UN Secretary-General and UNPROFOR, 'all necessary measures, through the use of air power, in and around the safe areas in the Republic of Bosnia and Herzegovina, to support UNPROFOR in the performance of its mandate'.[27] This tortuous language reflected equivocation among the leading members of the Security Council about the extent to which they were prepared to become directly involved in the conflict.

For the UN and NATO, the problem of protecting the six 'safe areas' was compounded by the fact that these were not neutral zones, but areas in which, and from which, Bosnian forces operated. The Serbs complained continuously that the so-called 'safe areas' were being used by the Bosnians to launch attacks against them, as was conspicuously the case with the Bosnian offensive launched from Bihac in November 1994. The Bosnian government cannot be blamed for its desire to maintain armed forces in the 'safe areas'; it naturally saw these forces as having a role both defending the areas, and in military operations aimed at ending their encirclement.

A further problem for the UN and NATO was the high degree of uncertainty about when and how force was to be used. Should it be used whenever the safe areas were attacked or humanitarian convoys stopped, even if the Bosnian armed forces had been engaged in attacks launched from the safe areas? And should the use of force be confined to the smoking guns directly implicated in attacks on the 'safe areas', or be directed more generally at Bosnian Serb military assets? These questions were especially hard to answer since any use of force required the agreement both of NATO and of Boutros-Ghali's representative in former Yugoslavia, Yasushi Akashi. The latter's extreme caution regarding the use of force seemed to be unhappily vindicated when such uses of force as did take place led to Serb retaliation in the form of taking UNPROFOR personnel hostage. During 1994 and the first half of 1995, despite some successes, such as the establishment of the heavy weapons exclusion zone around Sarajevo, no convincing answers were found. From the outset of the 'safe areas'concept, there were concerns (already articulated by Under-Secretary-General Kofi Annan on 4 June 1993 in a message seeking clarification of UNSCR 836) that the use of air-power would have serious security implications for personnel engaged in humanitarian assistance.

In mid-1995, Bosnian Serb arrogance made possible the emergence of an effective policy. By virtually stopping UN operations in Serb-held areas, including humanitarian aid to the safe areas, the Serbs effectively reduced UNPROFOR's vulnerability to reprisals. Then, by committing appalling atrocities in connection with the conquest of Srebrenica and Zepa in July 1995, they exposed the bankruptcy of existing Western and UN policies. Responding to what was both a humanitarian disaster and an affront to their credibility, the UN and NATO had to move towards decisive military action against the Serbs.

Overall, the experience of special protection areas suggests that preventing military activity within them is extremely difficult. In refugee camps there has often been coercive pressure on inmates from armed groups, whether inside or outside the camp. Areas of special protection may be used by one party as a springboard for military attacks, as in Bosnia-Herzegovina in 1993–95.

Sometimes the outside bodies which have designated certain areas as safe may have to take military action to make them so. In such cases, humanitarian considerations may point to the need to take sides in the conflict, at least to the extent of punishing and deterring those who violate safe areas. Humanitarian concerns can thus be part of the ratchet-like process whereby large international bodies are slowly goaded from the sidelines of conflicts, until they end up as active participants.

Trusteeship and Other Administrative Roles
A logical consequence of the international community's increased emphasis on humanitarian action might well be the establishment of temporary trustee-type administrations in areas undergoing social and

political breakdown. Such administrations might be established with the consent of local parties, or in a framework of coercive 'humanitarian intervention'.

In countries where the UN has become involved in peacekeeping and humanitarian activities because of a general breakdown of government, the organisation and its leading members have been reluctant to assume responsibility for government. For the most part such UN roles in government have been confined to administrative assistance, civil affairs programmes, training, helping to hold or monitor elections, and generally giving advice.

Former Yugoslavia is a clear case in point. The UN Secretariat was consistently reluctant to adopt any of the various plans advanced for administering Sarajevo even after a proper peace agreement was reached. This view was reinforced by the problems encountered by the EU Administrator for Mostar, who assumed his difficult responsibilities on 23 July 1994, in the wake of the US-brokered peace agreement between the Bosnian government and Bosnian Croats of February–March.

In some countries where government scarcely exists, or is itself part of the problem, limited roles of the type that the UN has assumed in recent operations may be inadequate. The absence of direct administrative responsibility may sometimes restrict the options available to UN forces to primarily military ones.

A major difficulty is that the historical record of various forms of mandate, trusteeship and international administration has been mixed. Iraq and Rwanda, both of which were under trusteeship for substantial periods in the first half of this century, serve as reminders that trusteeship is no simple cure-all. However, proposals for such arrangements have continued to appear in international diplomacy, and the concept certainly merits reconsideration.[28]

There is no sign of any new formal system of trusteeship. In some respects an imperial situation exists today, but who are the imperialists? Except in cases of regional hegemony, old-fashioned direct exercise of dominance is out of fashion. The UN Trusteeship Council, by ending the special status of Palau, has completed its last remaining task. While there may in some circumstances be good reasons to establish a temporary externally based administrative system, especially when such a proposal has the active support of all parties in a dispute, the probability is that, if this is done at all, it will be done indirectly, by the accretion of functions to various UN or other agencies and forces in a particular country and not by the proclamation of a new general system of trusteeship.

Implementing the Laws of War

One branch of humanitarian consideration that has come into sharp focus in recent conflicts is the laws of war. This body of law – also known as the 'rules of war' (a term often used within armed forces), and as 'international humanitarian law' (a term generally taken to encompass a wide range of human-rights instruments) – is intended to guide the conduct of belligerents and occupying powers, and to ensure particularly that certain basic rules are observed, including helping the wounded, proper treatment of prisoners, respect for inhabitants of occupied territories, and non-use of prohibited means and methods of warfare. It also deals with such enduring issues as the rights and duties of neutral powers.

Many formal provisions in the laws of war covering implementation and enforcement have been little used. For example, there have been relatively few cases of belligerents appointing protecting powers, which are supposed to perform such tasks as looking after the interests of civilians in occupied territories and facilitating the establishment of hospital zones. The provisions in the four 1949 Geneva Conventions for trial or extradition of offenders have scarcely been invoked, and no use at all has so far been made of the International Humanitarian Fact Finding Commission, set up in 1991 in accord with the terms of the 1977 Geneva Protocol I. All this does not mean the Conventions have not been implemented, but rather that implementation has often assumed different forms from what was originally envisaged.[29]

In the main conventions there is extensive provision for ICRC and other bodies to carry out a wide range of humanitarian and monitoring tasks, and in most conflicts it has been ICRC representatives who have done so, especially visiting places of detention and assisting with exchanges of prisoners. Belligerents are willing to entrust ICRC with such tasks partly because it is recognised as an independent and neutral intermediary. The combined emphasis on confidentiality and on host government consent which governs much of ICRC's work has been a strength as well as a weakness – a strength, because it allowed access to places where others could not go; but a weakness, because in the many cases where it was aware of infractions of the conventions, it could do relatively little. Over the past two or three decades ICRC has increasingly reminded belligerents of their obligations under the conventions and has issued public protests at particularly outrageous actions. In former Yugoslavia, ICRC publicly denounced ill-treatment of detainees and civilians on 23 August 1992, when ICRC was denied access to the Manjaca and Omarska camps, and on 7 September 1994, after the belligerents, despite repeated appeals from ICRC, continued to disregard the security of civilians.[30] In summary, ICRC can help implementation of the conventions, but it does not have (and indeed has never sought) a capacity to enforce them; that remains the responsibility of states.[31]

Since the mid-1980s, the UN has become more involved in enforcing provisions of international humanitarian law. Evidence of this growing role includes the following:

- In the **Iran–Iraq War**, the UN Secretary-General, acting on his own behalf, dispatched a mission to the area in January 1985 to investigate the conditions under which POWs were being held.

  On 21 March 1986, a UN Security Council statement for the first time criticised Iraq by name for using gas.[32] On 26 August 1988, the Security Council unanimously adopted Resolution 620 condemning 'the use of chemical weapons in the conflict between Iran and Iraq'.

- In the **Iraq–Kuwait conflict**, from August 1990 onwards, several UN Security Council resolutions criticised Iraqi violations of international humanitarian law, including seizure of hostages, in occupied Kuwait.

  UNSCR 674 of 29 October 1990 invited states to collect information on grave breaches by Iraq and make it available to the Security Council.

  After the suspension of hostilities on 28 February 1991 the Security Council took no further action on this front. However, its Resolution 686 of 2 March 1991 did require Iraq to accept liability for loss, damage or injury arising from its invasion and occupation of Kuwait.

- In the **wars in former Yugoslavia**, UNSCR 764 of 13 July 1992 reaffirmed that all parties are bound to comply with their obligations under international humanitarian law, and that persons who commit or order the commission of grave breaches are individually responsible.

  UNSCR 771 of 13 August 1992 called on states to collate substantiated information on violations of humanitarian law, and also said that if the parties failed to comply the Council would take 'further measures'.

UNSCR 780 of 6 October 1992 asked the Secretary-General to establish an impartial Commission of Experts, which was done that same month.

UNSCR 808 of 22 February 1993 established an international tribunal regarding violations of international humanitarian law in former Yugoslavia since 1991.

UNSCR 827 of 25 May 1993 approved the Statute of the International Tribunal for the Prosecution of Persons Responsible for Serious Violations of International Humanitarian Law Committed in the Territory of the Former Yugoslavia Since 1991, which was subsequently established in The Hague.

- In **Somalia**, UNSCR 794 of 3 December 1992 made several references to international humanitarian law, deploring widespread violations and stating that it 'strongly condemns all violations of international humanitarian law occurring in Somalia, including in particular the deliberate impeding of the delivery of food and medical supplies essential for the survival of the civilian population, and affirms that those who commit or order the commission of such acts will be held individually responsible'. This was the resolution that authorised the US-led UNITAF to intervene in Somalia; citing violations of international humanitarian law as part of the justification for intervention was unusual.

- Over **Rwanda**, UNSCR 918 of 17 May 1994 requested the Secretary-General 'to present a report as soon as possible on the investigation of serious violations of international humanitarian law committed in Rwanda during the conflict'.

UNSCR 955 of 8 November 1994 approved the Statute of the International Tribunal for Rwanda.

Apart from the UN Security Council, other international bodies have been increasingly preoccupied with issues relating to the implementation, or failure to implement, international humanitarian law. This was an important aspect of two cases taken to the International Court of Justice. The first was *Nicaragua v. USA*, on which judgment was given on 27 June 1986. This case concerned the legitimacy of planting mines in Nicaraguan waters, but also involved a number of other issues of the laws of war. The second was the case brought by Bosnia and Herzegovina against the Federal Republic of Yugoslavia (FRY), *Case Concerning the Application of the Convention on the Prevention and Punishment of the Crime of Genocide.*

One call for more effective implementation of international humanitarian law was the International Conference on the Protection of War Victims, held in Geneva from 30 August to 1 September 1993. Representatives of 160 states attended. Like the 1989 Paris Conference on Chemical Weapons, this tried to restore the sanctity of battered norms. Virtually all the recommendations in the declaration agreed at the conference were aimed at increasing the number of formal adherents to the existing rules of international humanitarian law and improving the dissemination and practical implementation of those rules.

Thus, since the mid-1980s there has been an exceptional amount of high-level activity designed to improve the implementation of the laws of war. In particular, the UN Security Council has acquired a greater role than was foreseen in the conventions themselves. This has proved extremely problematical. It has required the UN to uphold standards in circumstances where it cannot ensure their application.

Several conflicts, especially in former Yugoslavia and Rwanda, have compelled UN peacekeeping forces and international humanitarian agencies to confront the issue of how to act when they have evidence of massive violations of the most basic humanitarian rules by belligerents. Inasmuch as an answer has emerged, it appears to be that information on violations may be recorded and passed on, at least by some national contingents through their own national authorities, and through humanitarian workers. However, in some cases there have been understandings that such information would not be used or be the basis for formal evidence without further consultation.

In former Yugoslavia, despite the establishment of the International Criminal Tribunal in 1993, UN peacekeepers were not given a formal mandate to arrest suspected war criminals and hold them for possible trial, nor did they actually do so. Indeed, many UNPROFOR reports played down the war crimes issue. Clearly there would be some built-in problems for peacekeepers if they were expected to negotiate with belligerents on a wide range of matters (such as allowing the transit of relief convoys and helping arrange a peace settlement), while at the same time they were asked to arrest the same belligerents on war crimes charges. The Dayton Agreement of November–December 1995 contained specific commitments about the prosecution of war crimes. The establishment of the NATO-led Implementation Force (IFOR) in Bosnia in December raised hopes that suspected war criminals would be arrested. Yet IFOR was not given orders to pursue this matter actively.

Maintaining a precarious peace between belligerents seemed to have priority over forceful implementation of humanitarian norms. IFOR inherited UNPROFOR's dilemmas.

The issue of punishment of war crimes exposes the continuing tension between the power of states and non-state entities on the one hand, and ideas of an over-arching international order on the other. For most of the time the laws of war, like other parts of international law, must be implemented through national mechanisms of various kinds – national laws, manuals of military law, government-established commissions of inquiry, and courts and courts-martial. The weaknesses of relying on national implementation are notorious, and the record of non-state entities in applying the laws of war is even more problematic. Yet the point has not been reached where implementation on a supra-national level is proven. The establishment of the international tribunals for Yugoslavia and Rwanda is a significant step in that direction.

Concern about implementing international humanitarian law is a driving force behind proposals for the establishment of a permanent international criminal court, which is the subject of ongoing negotiations under UN auspices. There is no disagreement that this international court would be involved in trying three 'core crimes' – war crimes, crimes against humanity and genocide. However, there are numerous issues yet to be resolved about jurisdiction over other crimes, and the extent to which the prosecutor might have an independent investigatory role. Whether or not the champions of this proposal overcome the concerns of states about independent supra-national investigations into their security activities, the demand for effective implementation of the laws of war is likely to remain very strong, and to be difficult to translate into effective policies of international enforcement against recalcitrant states.

IV. KEY ISSUES

Attempts to carry out humanitarian missions in war situations have repeatedly highlighted certain inter-connected issues – impartiality, reconciling humanitarianism and human rights, possible prolongation of wars, accountability of humanitarian organisations, humanitarian problems of international economic sanctions, humanitarian assistance and development assistance as rivals, armed protection of humanitarian workers, and legal protection for peacekeeping forces and humanitarian workers.

Impartiality and Neutrality of Humanitarian Work
The concepts of impartiality and neutrality have for over a century been central to most approaches to humanitarian action in war. ICRC exemplifies this tradition. In its definition, the principle of impartiality means that the Red Cross 'makes no discrimination as to nationality, race, religious beliefs, class or political opinions. It endeavours to relieve the suffering of individuals, being guided solely by their needs, and to give priority to the most urgent cases of distress.' The principle of neutrality is defined thus: 'In order to continue to enjoy the confidence of all, the Red Cross may not take sides in hostilities or engage at any time in controversies of a political, racial, religious or ideological nature.'[1]

Impartiality and neutrality have also, for over a century, been the foundation of the international legal protection of humanitarian action in war. As the 1977 Geneva Protocol I states, 'relief actions which are humanitarian and impartial in character and conducted without any adverse distinction shall be undertaken, subject to the agreement of the Parties concerned in such relief actions. Offers of such relief shall not be regarded as interference in the armed conflict or as unfriendly acts'.[2]

For ICRC in particular, a reputation for impartiality, independence and neutrality is essential if it is to act in war zones, and to perform such delicate tasks as visiting people under internment, negotiating the release of POWs, and organising medical transport. The same is true, if to a slightly lesser degree, of many other humanitarian organisations.

Yet the idea of impartiality and neutrality has been under particular threat in the 1990s. Some of the problems are familiar. In wartime, humanitarian action, whether organised on its own or in conjunction with other measures, may seem impartial and disinterested to the outsiders engaging in it, but can be viewed differently by the local forces. History suggests that such efforts can seldom be perceived as impartial for any length of time. There are particular problems when, as so often happens in war, one party perceives the other not just as an aggressor, but as a ruthless or even genocidal power seeking to prevent humanitarian assistance reaching the victims of aggression. In such circumstances, one party may view another as simply not entitled to humanitarian assistance, and may act accordingly.

In civil wars, which have been the main form of conflict since 1945, the difficulties confronting a relief operation are especially great. Combatants' perceptions of neutrality become the practical measure of neutrality. Since rival communities are often very close physically and may aim at uprooting civilians, each community may be particularly aware of, and hostile to, any aid or protection accorded to its enemies.[3] An international relief presence often puts money into the hands of warlords, involves a degree of recognition of them as 'the authorities' in a particular area, and may act as a deterrent to air strikes against them.

The involvement of governments and major international political organisations in humanitarian action has added to the problems of maintaining impartiality and neutrality. NGOs working in conflict situations are often the channel by which governments, international organisations and major foundations distribute their humanitarian aid. Many such NGOs naturally fear that there may be political pressure on them to act in a way that would weaken their impartiality, or that mere association with a particular source of funding could be damaging.

The sheer scale of humanitarian action, and the involvement of governments and international organisations in financing it, have led it to be used as a means of achieving political objectives. This accusation was made regarding the situation in Georgia up to 1995:

> To date, efforts to use humanitarian instruments to facilitate normalisation have been dysfunctional. Attempts to achieve the rapid return of the internally displaced populations before conditions were conducive jeopardised their security and set back the peace process. Denial of assistance to insurgent regions by UN and other aid agencies has had serious negative consequences for their populations while doing little to push Abkhaz and Osset leaders to compromise in the political negotiations. In short, politicisation of humanitarian action – itself a departure from humanitarian principles – has undercut the attainment of humanitarian objectives.[4]

The need to secure some form of physical protection in war zones for aid workers, their activities and those they seek to assist presents a major challenge to impartiality and neutrality. The importance of such protection has been increasingly recognised by many involved in humanitarian work. Yet it is impossible to obtain such protection and maintain traditional views of this work as being above, or at least outside, the fray. Such protection – whether from local, external, multinational or even UN-authorised forces – jeopardises the impartiality and neutrality of aid efforts. Even if the forces involved are multinational and under UN auspices, they may be seen as favouring one side, especially if the UN is simultaneously involved in such political issues as enforcing sanctions, or trying to resolve the conflict.

A further, closely related challenge to impartiality and neutrality derives from the fact that many aid workers, as in Rwanda and Bosnia, may come to take a partisan view about the causes of a conflict, may protest publicly about atrocities, and may develop strong sympathies or antipathies to the parties. They may be particularly inclined to do so if outside states and international organisations have themselves offered no more than a humanitarian response. In the 1990s, international humanitarian agencies and NGOs have sometimes advocated major shifts in public policies, including even military intervention by outside powers or the creation of a new administration in a country. It is natural for them to want the international community to devote major human, military and financial resources to such purposes. In Bosnia and Rwanda, for example, many aid workers argued that there should have been a much more forceful UN role against the main groups engaged in mass killings – the Serbs in the former, the Hutu governmental forces in the latter.

Articulating policy in this way is inevitably controversial. Relief organisations have been criticised for making 'extraordinarily bold calls, apparently unimpeded by limits on their mandate and expertise, or by accountability'.[5] However, bold policy articulation represents, to some, an escape from a strait-jacket. The requirements of impartiality and neutrality have often led humanitarian organisations (and those in charge of peacekeeping operations) to describe conflicts in excessively bland or even misleading terms. Equally, when dependent on the cooperation of the predominant force in an area, humanitarian organisations have sometimes avoided systematic criticism of its crimes or failures. In Ethiopia in the late 1980s, for example, despite the evidence that repeated humanitarian crises were caused largely by disastrous government policies, ongoing civil war, and the absence of institutions through which changes could be introduced, 'a political emergency was redefined as a natural disaster'.[6] There is also pressure on humanitarian organisations to present the recipients of their assistance as 'deserving poor', worthy of their donors' generosity. Hence there can be a tendency to underestimate the extent to which, for example, certain refugee camps are filled by criminals or dominated by armed gangs.

Another reason why aid workers have become increasingly outspoken is the failure of major powers to develop clear and coherent policies themselves. Indeed, the very retreat of major powers into the bland language of humanitarianism has forced aid workers to advocate policy. David Bryer has wryly said of humanitarian organisations operating in Bosnia, 'by filling a policy vacuum, we have been elevated into political actors ourselves ... While NGOs have taken on some functions which were previously the ambit of states or inter-governmental bodies, the humanitarian response has often been the only meaningful expression of governments' concern'.[7] He has added a more general explanation of why NGOs sometimes advocate controversial policy positions:

Is it not that the 'complex emergencies' of this decade have held up a critical mirror to the previous professional compartments of emergency aid, development, security, human rights and international relations? They have shown us that it is impossible either to understand or to relieve such suffering without placing emergency aid – however 'impartial' – into a wider strategy, which *inter alia* enables the recipients of such aid to have protection. It is not the task of aid agencies to provide that protection, beyond cooperating with official and NGO human rights bodies when they have evidence of abuses, but it is incumbent on them to articulate what other actors could do to provide that protection. To take extreme examples, if NGOs come to advocate any use of military forces, it is only as a last resort, but it is not outside the interest in political and security issues which they now see as relevant. The greater recognition that providing aid can do harm as well as good makes many NGOs judge that they should not give that aid if they do not also press those who can reduce or prevent its abuse.[8]

The need for 'governments to address the policy vacuum' was emphasised by the International Federation of the Red Cross and Red

Crescent Societies at its 1995 International Conference. However, the movement seemed to envisage that the function of governmental action is 'to underpin humanitarian assistance whose independence and impartiality is respected and guaranteed', and to provide 'humanitarian space'.[9] In reality, humanitarian action itself often involves elements of partiality; and for governments to address policy vacuums often involves forging alliances between local parties, supporting one side or opposing another, and encouraging temporary or permanent withdrawals of exposed humanitarian workers.

The fact that some humanitarian actions have involved departures from traditional principles of non-partisanship has had one obvious consequence; it has led those organisations most anxious to retain a reputation for impartiality and neutrality to be circumspect in their relations with their more outspoken or engaged counterparts. ICRC has exemplified most clearly the concern that associating its work with that of others may undermine its impartiality. It has vigorously objected to the abuse of the Red Cross symbol by other humanitarian organisations. It has also pointed out that humanitarian work with political organisations, even as universal as the UN, contains pitfalls for the unwary. As the President of ICRC said in an address to the UN General Assembly in November 1992:

...humanitarian endeavour and political action must go their separate ways if the neutrality and impartiality of humanitarian work is not to be jeopardised ... it is dangerous to link humanitarian activities aimed at meeting the needs of victims of a conflict with political measures designed to bring about the settlement of the dispute between the parties.[10]

It is undeniably difficult for the UN, and for agencies within the UN system, to maintain impartiality when the system is by nature involved in a wide range of political decision-making, and when its security responsibilities may lead it to advocate enforcement measures against a particular party. This consideration, as well as the complex and cumbersome character of UN structures, has led some to conclude that the UN should not be in the humanitarian relief business at all. As James Ingram, Executive Director of WFP from 1982 to 1992, has stated:

The question arises whether humanitarian goals may not be better achieved under a new and different regime. I believe they would. The United Nations should confine its role to political functions associated with the resolution of disputes, the prevention of conflict and coercive interventions to end it. Reaching and succouring the victims of conflict and coordinating the relief efforts of the international community should cease to be a United Nations responsibility.[11]

Ingram proposes instead that the humanitarian goal of saving lives should be performed by an enlarged and internationalised ICRC, or else by a new organisation established by governments, preferably outside the UN framework. These proposals are not likely to be implemented. The political pressures in the UN system militate in favour of its involvement in this field, and despite all the difficulties some UN agencies have developed impressive skills and reputations. However, these proposals do usefully focus attention on the unavoidable conflicts between the UN's political and impartial humanitarian roles.

Can the principles of impartiality and neutrality stand up to the weight of the manifold challenges? These principles have had strong reaffirmation in the Red Cross movement's 1994 Code of Conduct for relief workers (discussed further below), and also in the Madrid Declaration of representatives of prominent humanitarian agencies and donors, drawn up at a 'humanitarian summit' on 14 December 1995. The Madrid Declaration did state bluntly that 'humanitarian assistance is neither a solution nor a panacea for crises which are essentially man-made'. It also reaffirmed a commitment 'to protect and feed the victims'. However, neither of these statements explored how protection was to be achieved. They avoided a simple truth, namely that if the provision of physical protection within conflict zones is seen as a necessary part of humanitarian action, then sometimes it may be necessary to have alliances with powers and even with local parties. The failure to bite this bullet may at times involve humanitarian workers betraying and abandoning those whom they seek to assist.

Tension Between Humanitarianism and Human Rights
One point of concern in many instances of humanitarian action has been the apparent clash with human rights. Because it is deemed to require impartiality humanitarian activity has frequently avoided political issues, even in cases involving fundamental human rights. The dichotomy between humanitarianism and human rights, always problematic, has been challenged in the post-Cold War era. Some NGOs concerned with human rights have made trenchant criticisms of the even-handedness, tentativeness and ineffectual character of many UN

peacekeeping and humanitarian activities. Human Rights Watch, a US-based organisation, said in a 1993 report:

> While severe human rights abuses often play a critical part in fueling armed conflict and aggravating humanitarian crisis, they have been given a low priority by the officials who oversee UN field operations. This lost agenda handicaps the UN in its new and ambitious undertakings, as it sells short one of the central ideals on which the UN was founded.[12]

Similarly, in a striking and occasionally strident critique of the role of humanitarian bodies in the conflicts of the 1990s, London-based African Rights has identified what it terms 'the basic dilemma':

> During the Cold War, a small and sharply-circumscribed space was labelled 'humanitarian'. The space was defined by Western governments and host governments, in ways that suited their political interests. Currently, there is a sharpened awareness of the problems of operating relief programmes under authorities (governments, rebel armies and militias) that are abusing human rights. These are old problems, but now there is the possibility to talk openly about them, and perhaps even to change operating practices. The central dilemma is whether it is possible to supply humanitarian assistance, under the auspices of a governing authority that abuses human rights, without also giving undue assistance to that authority, and hence doing a disservice to the people one is aiming to help.[13]

This publication, 'Humanitarianism Unbound?', itemises various ways in which relief has become intimately involved in insurgency and counter-insurgency warfare, the struggle for state power, and warlordism: material assistance to the combatants; providing strategic protection, for example by keeping roads open for both humanitarian and military traffic; and providing legitimacy to the controlling authority in any of a wide variety of ways, including, for example, disguising forced relocation to protected sites as a humanitarian relief operation. Humanitarian operations can also let governments off the hook from their own responsibilities for looking after the populations under their control. Humanitarian agencies are specifically accused of denying a case of forced resettlement in Ethiopia in 1988, despite the fact that their own staffs witnessed it.[14]

Sometimes humanitarian relief is seen as a weak substitute for human rights. In the 1990s, relief aid has been directed towards countries undergoing civil war in order to contain the outflow of refugees. In the process, norms have shifted from the right to asylum, and the right to leave one's country, to far more nebulous concepts such as 'in-country protection'. Providing relief can easily become a substitute for protecting persecuted people.

There is undeniably some tension between humanitarian and human-rights approaches, which seem to call for different and apparently incompatible policies – the first, for impartial delivery of relief, and the second, for robust opposition to those who violate human-rights norms. Yet there is no point in 'a fruitless theoretical argument about whether rights to humanitarian assistance or protection from violence are more important'.[15] Practice has shown that there is some scope for overlap. The UN has incorporated a human-rights element into some of its peacekeeping operations, especially its contributions to post-war reconstruction after the long civil wars in Cambodia and El Salvador. UNHCR has tried to combine its humanitarian action with a human-rights dimension, especially in drawing attention to gross violations in former Yugoslavia; its right to do so has not been questioned.[16] The process of bringing human rights, especially protection from violence, into humanitarian activities reinforces the conclusion that in practice humanitarian and political activities cannot be completely separated.

Possible Prolongation of Wars

Does the provision of humanitarian assistance during a war actually prolong it? This accusation has been made with particular frequency in connection with the wars in Ethiopia in the 1980s, and Somalia, Bosnia, Liberia and Sierra Leone in the 1990s. Of Ethiopia, for example, African Rights has said, 'There is little doubt that aid to the government side prolonged the war'.[17]

It is a truth not denied by any of the major humanitarian agencies involved in these conflicts that, despite serious efforts to prevent such an outcome, a proportion of aid does end up in the hands of the warring parties. Some may be taken at established checkpoints, as dues paid to ensure its onward passage; some may be stolen at gunpoint. Even if what is safely delivered is given only to civilians, some of them may pass it on to soldiers; the net effect in any case may be to release food, fuel or other supplies for use by the armed forces.

Thus humanitarian aid may provide a cushion which enables armies to carry on fighting; it may also enable losing sides to avoid admitting defeat, since they are protected from the pain and loss of life which might cause them to sue for peace. A dependency culture could emerge, in which a society relied heavily on aid, saw its own agriculture and industry weakened by an influx of foreign aid that undermined local market mechanisms, and was unable to end the fighting that had originally created the need for aid.

Actual cases frequently reveal quite different patterns. Since, in most conflicts, armies are the last groups to suffer starvation, the importance of food aid seeping through to them is often marginal. Frequently the provision of humanitarian assistance is merely neutral, enabling non-combatants to survive, but not fundamentally affecting the duration let alone the outcome of a war.

It may be impossible to know how long a war would have continued in the absence of such an effort, but even if aid were to prolong a war, that would not in itself prove that the effect of the aid was entirely negative. For example, in Bosnia and Herzegovina the humanitarian aid could conceivably have helped belligerents, and in particular the Bosnian government forces, to soldier on. Yet coupled with peace-keeping efforts, it also assisted in substantially reducing war-related deaths in Bosnia, especially in 1993 and 1994. Thus the war may have lasted longer but been less costly. In addition, the aid may have helped stave off what could otherwise have been a Bosnian defeat in the face of Serb offensives and harsh winters under siege. Finally, it helped to keep Bosnia in international focus, and contributed to the emergence in 1995 of a more active Western policy towards the conflict.

If humanitarian aid may on occasion prolong wars, the refusal to provide aid may provoke them. The spectacle of those who have the capacity to assist choosing not to do so can have huge emotional power. It is the humanitarian equivalent of the Red Army camped on the east bank of Vistula while the 1944 Warsaw uprising was brutally suppressed by the Germans.[18] The UK's fanatical adherence to *laissez-faire* during the 'great famine' in Ireland in 1845–49, and its refusal to take administrative or humanitarian measures to save lives, left an enduring legacy of bitterness.[19] This is still contributing to violence and distrust over a century later. The international community can hardly wish the twenty-first century to witness any repetition of this dismal experience on a global scale.

Accountability and Codes of Conduct

Many of the NGOs and relief agencies involved in humanitarian action make decisions about the fates of thousands of people, provide a flow of information about crisis situations and, increasingly, engage in policy advocacy. Yet they are not always fully accountable for their actions. Also, the codes of conduct under which they operate are proving problematic.

In the country where operations take place there is often an absence of formal controls. In failing or failed states, for example, there may be no functioning ministries to regulate programmes, no labour legislation to constrain hiring and firing policies, and no structures to enforce demands for local financial accountability. 'In this case, the power relations between host and NGO are dramatically tilted in favour of the latter – and the hosts sometimes resort to the power of the gun to re-assert their influence, in a malign way'.[20]

Furthermore, there is often a lack of serious, publicly available professional analysis of the impact of humanitarian action. Those engaged in relief actions know of cases in which the wrong types of goods were sent, distribution was woefully mismanaged, or grain supplies arrived late but just in time to destroy the market in local produce, thus exacerbating problems of dependency. The proliferation of new NGOs with little or no professional expertise has been a particular concern.

The major players do train their personnel and do have procedures for assessing the needs of victims and the impact of their action. However, there remains a case for developing higher professional standards, fuller accountability, and more open public debate about the roles of international agencies and NGOs. The distribution of humanitarian relief must be viewed as an activity that requires professional management and evaluation.

A ten-point Code of Conduct for relief workers, drawn up in 1994 and unanimously approved by representatives of 142 governments in December 1995, and also endorsed by over 70 NGOs, sought to address problems of ethics and accountability. 'Aid is given regardless of race, creed or nationality of the recipients ... Aid priorities are calculated on the basis of need alone. We shall endeavour not to act as instruments of government foreign policy. We hold ourselves accountable to both those we seek to assist and those from whom we accept resources'.[21] Not one of the ten points addressed in any way the critical issue of how to

60

protect vulnerable populations and aid activities, nor how impartial relief work could be combined with human-rights advocacy, sanctions or other coercive measures. Governments and NGOs appeared to be addressing humanitarian issues in a pious and abstract manner far removed from the harsh dilemmas resulting from wars. The December 1995 Madrid Declaration was another reflection of this tendency.

It is easy to agree on such principles as accountability, but much harder to act on them. One critical account of humanitarian action in war is the five-volume Joint Evaluation of Emergency Assistance to Rwanda issued in 1996. This interesting exercise in accountability resulted from a multinational, multi-donor research effort, whose main objective was 'to draw lessons from the Rwanda experience relevant for future complex emergencies as well as for current operations in Rwanda and the region, such as early warning and conflict management, preparation for and provision of emergency assistance, and the transition from relief to rehabilitation and development'. The volume on humanitarian aid concluded unambiguously that 'humanitarian action cannot serve as a substitute for political, diplomatic and, where necessary, military action. The onus of responsibility must, first and foremost, be upon the political and diplomatic domain to address complex emergencies'. It also called on the UN Security Council to establish a Humanitarian Sub-Committee to 'inform fully the Security Council of developments and concerns regarding the humanitarian dimensions of complex emergencies'.[22] Its conclusions may be flawed – the discussion of protection is weak, and one more UN committee does not seem likely to transform the landscape – but the study is a welcome recognition that humanitarian action needs to be subject to thorough evaluation and accountability. As was stated in the study's conclusions, 'A tendency by some official agencies and NGOs to emphasise or inflate positive accomplishments and play down or ignore problems resulted in distorted reporting. Even basic data on staff, finances and activities were difficult or impossible to obtain from a number of NGOs'.[23]

Humanitarian Problems of International Economic Sanctions

International economic sanctions are often viewed in a favourable light because they constitute a form of international pressure that falls short of war. UN-authorised impositions of sanctions, rare until 1990, have increased greatly since. The main cases of UN sanctions since 1945 (with the principal authorising resolution in brackets) are listed below:

Table 4: Cases of UN sanctions since 1945

Year	Location Type of sanction (Authorising resolution)
1966–79	**Rhodesia** General economic sanctions, following its unilateral declaration of independence. (UNSCR 232 of 16 December 1966.)
1977–94	**South Africa** Embargo on the supply of arms on the grounds that their acquisition by South Africa constitutes a threat to international peace and security. (UNSCR 418 of 4 November 1977.)
1990–	**Iraq** General economic sanctions, following its invasion of Kuwait. (UNSCR 661 of 6 August 1990.)
1991–96	**Yugoslavia (and its successor states)** Arms embargo, following the outbreak of fighting. (UNSCR 713 of 25 September 1991.)
1992–	**Somalia** Arms embargo following outbreak of internal conflict. (UNSCR 733 of 23 January 1992.)
1992–	**Libya** Arms and air traffic embargo, following demands on Libya to renounce support for terrorism. More general sanctions were imposed in November 1993. (UNSCR 748 of 31 March 1992 and 883 of 11 November 1993.)
1992–96	**Federal Republic of Yugoslavia (Serbia and Montenegro)** General economic sanctions, following the FRY's military involvement in Bosnia and Herzegovina. (UNSCR 757 of 30 May 1992.)

1992–   **Liberia**
Arms embargo, following cease-fire violations. (UNSCR 788 of 19 November 1992.)

1992–   **Khmer Rouge-held areas of Cambodia**
Petroleum sanctions following failure of the Party of Democratic Kampuchea to comply with its obligations under the 1991 Paris agreements. (UNSCR 792 of 30 November 1992.)

1993–94   **Haiti**
Arms embargo and petroleum sanctions, owing to the refugee flows from Haiti, and the failure of the regime to restore the legitimate government. (UNSCR 841 of 16 June 1993.)

1993–   ***União Nacional para a Independência Total de Angola (UNITA)* rebel movement in Angola**
Arms embargo and petroleum sanctions following its failure to accept the results of elections and to observe a cease-fire. (UNSCR 864 of 15 September 1993.)

1994–   **Rwanda**
Arms embargo, following the continuing and systematic violence within the country. (UNSCR 918 of 17 May 1994.)

1996–   **Sudan**
Restrictions on Sudanese officials abroad and on aircraft movements following an assassination attempt against President Hosni Mubarak of Egypt. (UNSCR 1070 of 16 August 1996.)

While the humanitarian or other rationales for using sanctions as distinct from other forms of pressure are often persuasive, the experience of some of these cases suggests that there are conflicts between sanctions and humanitarianism. Frequently (as in the cases of Iraq in 1991 and Haiti in 1994) sanctions are preludes to measures involving the use of armed force. Further, ordinary citizens of the target state, especially the poor and the vulnerable, normally suffer the adverse effects of sanctions more than the government and its armed forces. Any sanctions based on the idea that domestic suffering will make people rise up against their government clearly conflict with humanitarian priorities. Finally, sanctions can, as in the case of Haiti, contribute to migration out of the sanctioned state.

In two of the major cases of general economic sanctions in the post-Cold War period – Iraq, and Serbia/Montenegro – the UN Security Council has made provision for exceptions on humanitarian grounds, for example, when there is a demonstrated need for food or medicine for vulnerable sections of the population. The imperatives that led to provision for possible exceptions were obviously overwhelming, yet the experience has left questions in the minds of those involved in managing such policies. If such humanitarian exceptions are permitted, they could reduce the suffering caused by the sanctions, and so weaken their already uncertain effects. A different and probably more serious concern is that the existence of humanitarian assistance is assumed by the Security Council to mean that there is a safety net under the vulnerable, when in fact humanitarian exceptions do not work well. The target state, as in the case of Iraq, may simply reject them, at the cost of huge suffering.[24] It may be difficult to justify humanitarian aid while simultaneously imposing sanctions, especially in view of the rhetoric of humanitarianism, which abhors political distinctions and asserts the impartiality of assistance efforts. The UNHCR Chief of Mission in Serbia and Montenegro, Judith Kumin, referred to 'a fundamental contradiction – trying to implement a humanitarian programme in a sanctions environment'.[25] If this contradiction was more widely understood, the Security Council, when imposing sanctions, would at least be making an informed decision reflecting the reality that humanitarian exceptions are likely to be limited and controversial, and the vulnerable will still suffer most.

Humanitarian Assistance versus Development Assistance
Economic and administrative failure can take as heavy a human toll as war. Poor nutrition, contaminated water supplies, inadequate health facilities and high unemployment can all cause massive human suffering and loss of life. They can also contribute to the breakdown of states and the outbreak of war. More lives might be saved by addressing these enduring problems in many countries than by concentrating so many resources on a limited number of war-torn countries. No-one disputes the truism that, where war is concerned, prevention is better than cure.

Humanitarian aid and development aid are sometimes seen as rival claimants for limited funds. In 1980, funding by governments for emergency humanitarian relief constituted less than 1.5% of total official development assistance (ODA) spending world-wide; in 1993 and 1994, it was about 10%. This is still a small part of the total, but has been enough to reinforce concern that there is increasing willingness to use humanitarian assistance as a foreign–policy tool, often in isolation from any long-term strategy.[26] There is often more than a suspicion that aid is channelled in a humanitarian direction because a particular war has caught the public's attention, rather than because of any well-considered plan for usefully spending funds. Aid for the developing countries of the 'South' has declined in the 1990s, being squeezed not only by the flow of funds to emergency humanitarian relief, but also by the demands of the post-communist countries for capital and assistance. Furthermore, the belief that effective economic development comes first from within societies themselves and that many externally supported development programmes, especially in some Cold War client states, have failed, is growing increasingly prevalent.

The rivalry between these two approaches is exacerbated by the fact that they have separate and to some extent rival organisational bases in the UN system. Also, humanitarian aid under UN auspices is sometimes associated with supranational interventionism, whereas economic development projects are generally conducted in close association with recipient governments. In addition, some humanitarian aid is criticised as a panic response to contain flows of refugees.

Despite these tensions, humanitarian assistance and development assistance need not be seen as rivals. Many organisations, from ICRC to Oxfam, do not limit their action to emergency assistance. Both organisations distribute seed and agricultural tools to enable people to recover a measure of self-sufficiency, and rehabilitation programmes make up a large part of their relief activities. In short, there is a continuum between emergency action and rehabilitation/development programmes.

Armed Protection
The role of military forces is now the most important single issue to address; there has been too little sustained discussion of this issue. Military assistance for humanitarian workers and military protection of vulnerable populations has expanded in the 1990s, and has taken many forms – not just full-scale humanitarian intervention or establishing

safety zones, but also the armed protection of convoys, and the maintenance of order in refugee camps. Those providing the armed protection have included not only UN peacekeeping forces, but also those of individual countries, and locally raised forces of an *ad hoc* character.

Some observers have seen a general pattern of military involvement in humanitarian action as natural, perhaps inevitable. Richard Connaughton, writing from a military perspective, has gone so far as to say:

> In a conflict environment, humanitarian organisations will increasingly look to the military, certainly in the early stages, for those capabilities which they themselves do not possess. These capabilities include the provision of security, protection, resources including transportation, the capacity to control and the provision of information.[27]

In practice, most international humanitarian organisations with conflict experience seek to distance themselves from 'the military', whether local or foreign, for as long as they can, and want a degree of control over the type of military support provided for their activities. Although in some situations many of them do have to rely on armed forces for assistance, the relationship with their protectors can be among the most problematic aspects of humanitarian action in war.[28] It can be open or covert, can involve favours and bribery, and often threatens the impartiality of humanitarian work. Some organisations, including ICRC, have come to see occasional recourse to armed escorts as a necessary stop-gap measure, which has its limitations and contradictions. It is no substitute for the hoped-for restoration of respect for the Red Cross emblem. They argue, persuasively, that as long as armed escorts are needed to protect their activities, there can be no realistic hope that belligerents will show respect for defenceless civilians and prisoners. However, in many conflicts the issue of protecting humanitarian workers and vulnerable populations is likely to require not only a hope that the belligerents will observe the rules of restraint, but also a preparedness to take action to encourage them to do so.

One key issue is the protection of the humanitarian workers themselves. The crises of the post-Cold War era have led to many proposals for providing armed protection to humanitarian workers, whether working for UN or for other agencies. The situation of such workers in Somalia before UNITAF's intervention in December 1992 was among the many frustrating and tragic experiences leading to such demands. The proposal received high-level support, including from UN Under-Secretary-General Jan Eliasson in February 1993:

Additional measures for respect of humanitarian aid and for protection of relief personnel are now necessary. The blue ensign of the United Nations and the symbols of the International Red Cross and Red Crescent, and of other relief agencies, no longer provide sufficient protection.[29]

Citing such concerns, Childers and Urquhart suggested setting up 'a separate and distinctive United Nations Humanitarian Security Police'.[30] Humanitarian personnel, they argued, might need protection before there is a UN military intervention, and might also need to keep some visible distance from UN military forces.

Some UN reports have suggested that some proposed national volunteer corps known in the organisation as 'white helmets' might not only support 'humanitarian relief, rehabilitation and technical cooperation for development activities', but also (at least potentially) provide 'with their presence a deterrent and a symbolic protective cover in their working relationship with humanitarian operators.' They are envisaged as having 'a reassuring effect' and becoming 'a component of security and safety in the rehabilitation stage of emergency operations'.[31]

Such a protective role would go far beyond that of the existing UN volunteers, with which the proposed 'white helmuts' are often, confusingly, associated. The UN volunteers, established in 1970, offer professional expertise, not protection. They operate under the UN Development Programme, and by 1994 numbered about 4,000. Increasingly since the 1980s, they have played a humanitarian assistance role, including in areas of conflict, and sometimes in conjunction with UN peacekeeping operations.[32] The UN General Assembly has passed resolutions in favour of the 'white helmets', but these have referred to their role in activities like those of the UN volunteers (humanitarian relief, rehabilitation, technical cooperation), not to their possible protective or deterrent function.[33]

The various proposals for a dedicated UN force to protect humanitarian operations have not moved towards a detailed operational plan. There are six considerations against such a force.
- The sheer scale and difficulty of the protection problem suggests the need for a much larger and more professional force than anything that has been envisaged to date.

- Since there are already precedents of UN peacekeepers and UN-authorised enforcement bodies specifically assisting humanitarian workers, it is not obvious that a new force would add much.
- In the major case where UN peacekeepers/enforcers were not acceptable – northern Iraq since 1991 – it was never likely that any other UN force (apart from the harmless UN Guards) would have been any more acceptable to Baghdad.
- The creation of a new force might complicate yet further the already Byzantine complexity of UN force structures in the field, especially if it was not under the authority of the Security Council.
- It could cause resentment in many host countries, either because it was considered unnecessary, or because the protection was provided only for the humanitarian workers, not for those they were there to help.
- Many humanitarian workers and organisations, both inside and out-side the UN system, do not want this particular kind of protection, which they view as unrealistic.

In the absence of any single model or organisational basis of protection, there was a marked trend in the early 1990s towards more, and more varied forms of, protection. The elements of failure in the armed protection of humanitarian work in Somalia in 1992–93 did not stop this trend.

Rwanda represents an extreme case of physical protection of threatened people (as distinct from, say, food aid) as the critical issue. In the Rwanda crisis of 1994 three military operations supported and protected humanitarian assistance, and also protected threatened populations – the UN peacekeeping operation UNAMIR, the French *Opération Turquoise*, and the US *Operation Support Hope* in the camps in eastern Zaire. These three operations, each with very different basic mandates, represent an evolution from UN-based multilateral force, the control of which was heavily criticised, to an operation led by a single country. *Operation Support Hope* was deliberately presented as entirely distinct from UN peacekeeping: 'This is not peacekeeping, it is an humanitarian operation'.[34]

Analyses of Rwanda by those involved in humanitarian aid have not always discussed the matter of protection consistently. The volume on aid in the Joint Evaluation of Emergency Assistance to Rwanda stated clearly in the main body of the text that 'the critical need was for security and physical protection', yet the 'Findings and Recom-mendations' failed to pick up this theme or to explore its implications. Instead, much attention was given to the intellectually easier, but arguably less important, question of whether delivery of aid by the military is more expensive than delivery by civilian aid organisations.[35]

Legal Protection for Peacekeepers and Humanitarian Workers

The idea that certain classes of people, such as those performing particular humanitarian services, should have a privileged position has always had a place in the laws of war. Treaties currently in force contain numerous provisions for the protection of religious and medical personnel, agents of relief societies, journalists and civil defence workers; and for respect for the Red Cross and UN emblems.[36]

UN peacekeeping troops, and also humanitarian workers, were in obvious danger in the conflicts of the early 1990s, and the number of casualties was higher than in earlier operations. Between 1948 and 1990 there were 398 fatalities in peacekeeping missions; between 1991 and August 1995 there were 456.[37] The worst year was 1993, largely because of events in Somalia. There was also an increase in ICRC fatalities – less than ten per annum in each of the years 1985–91, 18 in 1992, and 23 in 1993. However, there were none in 1994 and 1995.

When UN peacekeeping forces are involved in hostilities, are they to be regarded (at least for the purposes of the laws of armed conflict) simply as belligerents, on an equal footing with other parties? Or are they in some way in a superior position?[38] It is natural to want to give UN forces, and humanitarian workers, a privileged status. Many Security Council resolutions have already sought to secure respect for both peacekeeping personnel and humanitarian workers. In former Yugoslavia, a resolution in June 1992 demanded 'that all parties and others concerned cooperate fully with UNPROFOR and international humanitarian agencies and take all necessary steps to ensure the safety of their personnel'.[39] In Rwanda, a resolution in June 1994 demanded 'that all parties in Rwanda strictly respect the persons and premises of the United Nations and other organisations serving in Rwanda, and refrain from any acts of intimidation or violence against personnel engaged in humanitarian and peace-keeping work'.[40]

In December 1994, the UN General Assembly approved the text of the Convention on the Safety of UN and Associated Personnel. It was a response to the many cases of attacks on, and hostage-taking of, UN peacekeepers and those working for humanitarian organisations, and followed the many Security Council resolutions condemning such attacks and calling on parties to ensure the safety of such personnel. During the negotiating phase, humanitarian organisations expressed concern that the Convention would protect only those personnel who are

69

formally participating in a UN operation, as distinct from all humanitarian workers who may be assisting such an operation, or such
workers in conflicts where there is no UN operation. However, the final
text includes not only peacekeeping troops, but also humanitarian
workers with, for example, an NGO or a specialised agency, provided
they are part of an operation under UN authority and control.[41]

Can the new Convention on the Safety of UN Personnel be
implemented, or is it another case of the UN willing the end but not the
means? Article 11, echoing the 1949 Geneva Conventions, requires
states parties to follow an 'extradite or prosecute' rule regarding alleged
offenders – that is, those suspected of attacks on UN and associated
personnel. Thus, like so many treaties, the Convention relies heavily on
states being willing and able to take action against their own nationals.
If this does not work, what happens? The Delphic terms of Article 7(3)
appear to leave the matter to states. 'States Parties shall cooperate with
the United Nations and other States Parties, as appropriate, in the
implementation of this Convention, particularly in any case where the
host State is unable itself to take the required measures.' The
Convention does not directly address the possibility that UN peacekeeping forces might themselves take action against alleged offenders; if
they were to do so, UN forces could find themselves parties to an armed
conflict, in which case the convention would probably cease to apply at
that point, being replaced by the law of international armed conflict.[42]
This would imply an important transition of the status of a peacekeeping
operation, with broad policy ramifications.

The critically important issue of protecting peacekeepers and
humanitarian workers is becoming part of international law. (There are
also provisions for their protection in the Protocol on mines agreed in
1996, outlined below.) Yet there are risks in stressing their special legal
status. The humanitarian worker might end up involuntarily assuming
the role sometimes played by the missionary in the nineteenth century –
when attacked, providing a basis or at least an excuse for external
military action. There are also risks, all too obvious after the events in
Mogadishu in 1993, in calling those who oppose or threaten UN
personnel 'outlaws'. Special protection of peacekeepers and humanitarian workers, if not implemented with considerable caution and skill,
could be associated with a new kind of colonial mentality.

Anti-personnel Land-mines
Anti-personnel land-mines have rightly become a focus for much
humanitarian agitation and action. There are about 100m land-mines

scattered throughout 64 countries which are killing on average 30 people a day and injuring over 35, many of the casualties being children. They have necessitated huge and expensive efforts to de-mine affected areas, and to assist the many people maimed by mines.[43] The UN General Assembly has repeatedly called for states to adopt moratoria on the export of anti-personnel land-mines, and to agree to new prohibitions and restrictions on the use of such weapons.[44]

Within some major armies there has been extensive reconsideration of anti-personnel mine use. Prominent figures including General Norman Schwarzkopf have said that they serve no useful military purpose. A group of military experts convened by ICRC in February 1996 stated that the military value of land-mines as used in the past 55 years had received little attention in published military studies. They noted that establishing extensive minefields is time-consuming, expensive and dangerous, and that although anti-tank mines are militarily useful, anti-personnel mines are much less so.[45]

Anti-personnel land-mines are classic subjects for prohibitions under the laws of war, both because they are indiscriminate, and because they continue to cause damage after wars have ended. Protocol II of the 1981 Convention on Specific Conventional Weapons placed some limits on their use, but its effect has been minuscule, and it was not formally applicable in non-international armed conflicts. In May 1996 a review conference of parties to the 1981 Convention agreed to an 'Amended Protocol II', applying to internal as well as international conflicts, prohibiting the use of undetectable anti-personnel mines, placing restrictions on the use of other mines, and seeking to establish special protection for a wide range of UN, ICRC and other humanitarian missions.[46] Campaigners for the complete abolition of anti-personnel mines were disappointed that these gains were so limited.

On 5 October 1996, at a diplomatic conference in Ottawa, 50 countries (including the US, the UK, France, Japan, Germany and Iran) agreed to a declaration calling for a global ban on anti-personnel land-mines. Controlling this problem would be a major contribution to the cause of humanity in warfare. A complete prohibition of the production, sale and use of such weapons, although hard to enforce in many conflicts, would reduce the huge number of non-combatant and post-war casualties. International collaboration on mine removal is already developing, and should also be a priority of governments and armed forces.

V. COORDINATING HUMANITARIAN ACTION

The problem of coordinating the manifold and often competing actions of humanitarian organisations is not new. Even when few organisations are involved the coordination problems are daunting. These are especially difficult in civil wars: the number of belligerent parties, the disputes as to their status, the general social disorder, and the fast-moving character of events all create problems for humanitarian operations, and at the same time reinforce the need for coordination.

The UN has long had a practice whereby the Secretary-General designated in a particular country a specific UN agency as the 'lead agency' with overall responsibilities for humanitarian relief operations. In Cambodia, the lead agency was the United Nations Children's Emergency Fund (UNICEF). In former Yugoslavia (where the operation began shortly before Department of Humanitarian Affairs [DHA] was set up) it was, and remained, UNHCR. This 'lead agency' system has been challenged in the 1990s, including in several countries at war.

The Wide Range of Official and Unofficial Organisations

Many different organisations are involved in humanitarian work; each has its own special skills and capabilities, and the situations in which they act are different. They include local governmental bodies, aid and disaster relief agencies of individual foreign countries, and international organisations under UN or other auspices. They sometimes also include certain military formations, especially some UN peacekeeping or UN-authorised forces.

Beyond such official bodies there are literally thousands of relief agencies with very different structures, functions, and capacities, including local NGOs (which are commonly neglected elements of humanitarian relief efforts), and also NGOs operating internationally. Many NGOs are proud of their independence, and of their ability to act quickly. For example, the willingness of *Médecins sans Frontières* to act anywhere, without waiting for formal political agreement, has evoked much support, even though this group has had to withdraw from some impossibly dangerous situations, as in Somalia after the UN-backed UNITAF military intervention.

The large number of NGOs involved in humanitarian action in 'complex emergencies' can sometimes be a problem. In Bosnia, in the words of the Director of Oxfam, 'although the duplication of NGO activities in Bosnia has been kept to a minimum by the UNHCR taking a clear coordinating role, by December 1995 there were 279 international NGOs operating ... a figure which represents an almost fourfold increase over two years'.[1] In the Rwanda crisis in 1994, at least 200 NGOs were involved as well as many other international bodies; efforts at coordination were themselves numerous, varied and largely unsuccessful.[2]

It has been suggested that, within the UN system, the different and overlapping mandates of various agencies make effective responses impossible, that there is a need for overall strategic direction, for a clearer division of labour, or for greater coordination between them. Some have even said that their numbers should simply be reduced. As Gareth Evans has explained:

There are widely acknowledged inadequacies in the present UN international system, and structural reasons lie at the heart of them. In the first place, the post-Second World War relief system evolved from a structure created for different purposes. Apart from UNHCR and UNICEF, all the main agencies now involved in emergencies – i.e., WFP, UNDP [UN Development Programme], FAO [Food and Agriculture Organisation] and WHO [World Health Organisation] – acquired that role as a secondary function, the main role being seen as the promotion of economic and social development. Notwithstanding the dramatic upsurge in their humanitarian relief work in the 1980s, the organisation of the agencies underwent no fundamental change.[3]

The picture of a large number of agencies, within and beyond the UN system, designed for one set of problems and having trouble adapting to another set, is not altogether fair. Many agencies have moved gradually beyond their original purposes and have tackled other problems than those they were originally set up to address.

There have been several proposals to remedy this. These have included proposals for establishing a single consolidated UN body, for which various titles have been suggested, including UN Relief Agency, or UN Disaster Response Agency. This idea carries with it two main risks. First, all UN agencies go through periods of poor performance, so having all eggs in a single basket is unwise. Second, consolidating everything under one roof might only exacerbate the divide between humanitarian relief and economic development. In the end the UN has established the DHA with a modest coordinating role.

For UNHCR in particular, there are risks in being subordinated to a single consolidated UN body. UNHCR's core responsibilities are unique in that they are imposed by events outside the control of the its Executive Committee, the UN General Assembly and the Security Council. Whatever the financial and political climate, more refugees mean more work. Moreover, this responsibility is discharged on behalf of those who by definition have no government to which they can turn. In a single UN humanitarian agency these unique responsibilities, which at times require opposition to the wishes of governments, would inevitably be diluted at the refugees' expense.

Because the UN system has been so obviously over-stretched in a wide variety of humanitarian and peacekeeping roles, it might be logical to look to regional organisations of one kind or another to fill the gap. Such organisations vary enormously. Some, such as the European Union, have substantial resources and are developing expertise, for example through the European Community Humanitarian Office (ECHO). Other regional organisations (including the Commonwealth) are better suited to the tasks of mediation and conflict prevention than emergency humanitarian action.

The UN Department of Humanitarian Affairs
The UN has addressed the problem of a confusion of humanitarian activities by attempting to coordinate, not consolidate within a single agency. This effort is centred on the DHA, based in New York and Geneva. The DHA, set up in March 1992, was intended to have a key role within the UN system by providing early warnings of humanitarian disasters and coordinating action in the field. It has modest funds, including a Central Emergency Revolving Fund (CERF) to provide reimbursable advances to pay for emergency humanitarian action.[4]

The response to DHA has been mixed. Elements of coordination have developed. Under the DHA, an Inter-Agency Standing Committee (IASC) meets quarterly, with representation from the heads of key UN agencies, ICRC and the Federation of Red Cross Societies, and from three groups of NGOs. For particular countries in crisis there are now single-needs assessments. There are also the UN Consolidated Inter-Agency Humanitarian Assistance Appeals, though only one (that for former Yugoslavia) has been adequately funded since these appeals were introduced in 1992.[5]

Within some war-torn countries DHA coordination has made a difference. In Angola, where DHA was asked to provide a coordinating role in March 1993, 'almost every organisation involved in humanitarian assistance wanted coordination, albeit "light and not

74

bureaucratic"'. At the same time, however, DHA had 'to distance itself from the UN's political activities because Angolans, the government, and UNITA, perceived them as a failure.'[6] In several countries (for example Mozambique, Rwanda and Somalia), the DHA has appointed a Humanitarian Coordinator with overall responsibility for relief efforts. This is intended to replace the previous system of the 'lead agency'. Sometimes this has worked. As two NGOs have said:

> Our experience of working with UN agencies in emergencies is varied, but one thing we have learnt is that it is vital for the in-country UN authority to build a consensus among the various relief agencies and NGOs involved. In Mozambique, the Humanitarian Coordinator, whose authority is delegated from the Special Representative, has on the whole been able to do this.[7]

Inevitably, within the new system there are still many problems. The system of coordination is not fundamentally different from one instituted 20 years earlier, on the basis of General Assembly Resolution 2816 calling on the Secretary-General to appoint a Disaster Relief Coordinator. The DHA has few resources compared to the other agencies it is intended to coordinate. It has itself suffered from problems of coordination and continuity, due partly to being split between two sites (New York and Geneva), and having had no less than three directors in its four years of existence. It has no executive power to direct aid in a particular crisis. The idea of coordination does not itself address the wider problem of overlapping mandates of different agencies. Pressures for centralised and coordinated decision-making can reduce operational effectiveness and flexibility in the field. The role of individual states, especially donors (whether of finance or services), has not diminished, and adds a layer of complexity. It is significant that a key UN Secretariat decision in the humanitarian field – to evacuate UN personnel from the camps in eastern Zaire following the outbreak of fighting there in late October 1996 – was taken by the UN Security Coordinator in the Department of Administration and Management, in consultation with various officials and agencies, and not by DHA.

The emphasis on coordination within a country under a Humanitarian Coordinator does not itself solve the problem of crises which, as frequently happens, spill over frontiers and involve the territory of several states, nor does it solve the problem of relations with special envoys to a region, appointed by the UN Secretary-General. Somalia and Rwanda, baptisms of fire for the system, served as reminders that when problems on the ground are extremely difficult and the political responses to them are flawed, to expect a coordination system to achieve success is to expect miracles. In many conflicts in the former Soviet Union, too, the DHA has been unable to assume the central coordinating role that was originally envisaged. Indeed, where there are significant refugee flows and a major UNHCR presence, it is not realistic to expect that representatives of UNHCR with its substantial budgets and responsibilities, and a strong tradition of being a 'lead agency', will accept 'coordination' from a much less powerful and less experienced body such as DHA. There remains, as there was before, an element of personal chemistry and happenstance in whether the different aspects of a relief effort do or do not meld into an effective whole in a particular crisis.

A practical and political problem of the new system is the division of responsibilities in the field between the UNDP, concerned primarily with long-term development projects, and the DHA, concerned with emergency relief. There are genuine uncertainties about where their respective responsibilities end; the area of rehabilitation lies uneasily between development and relief. Also, many governments, especially in the Group of 77 (developing countries), are critical of the idea of a Humanitarian Coordinator for a particular country. They fear that this might involve meddling in their internal affairs. The fact that the appointment of a Humanitarian Coordinator is not subject to the *agrément* of the country concerned has strengthened such fears, reinforcing as it does the notion that humanitarian action and humanitarian intervention are intimately linked. There has been similar concern over the post of Emergency Relief Coordinator.[8]

Attempts to coordinate, including those taking place under DHA auspices, naturally receive a mixed response from some non-UN bodies, which could reasonably fear some loss of identity or capacity to act independently. ICRC, which is of course a special case, has participated in various DHA initiatives, but in that context has had to reiterate its independence and impartiality. ICRC has also been concerned that the UN, by concentrating on humanitarian action, risks abandoning its purportedly proper role in the international division of labour, which is to work on politico-military responses to conflicts.

Strengthening the coordination of humanitarian activities is politically sensitive and inherently difficult. In UN General Assembly debates on the matter on 23 and 25 November 1994, many Group of 77 states expressed reservations about the direction in which coordination had been moving. However, those involved in UN humanitarian operations in the field generally take the view that the most worrying problem is not coordination, but actual capacity. The inadequacy of resources, which reflects the limited character of states' commitment to humanitarian relief, remains the largest constraint on effective action. It is doubtful whether DHA is an improvement on the 'lead agency' approach, and whether it can endure in its present form.

Early Warning

A key element in any organisation's response to challenges is early warning. Such warning may be valuable if it can assist efforts to prevent crises, for example through diplomatic initiatives; indeed early warning is quite often considered a part of 'preventive diplomacy'.[9] However, early warning also has a role in the prompt and efficient delivery of humanitarian relief. Furthermore, an efficient system of warning has a crucial role to play in the perceived fairness of any system of relief.

If governments and international agencies simply react to the latest television reports, certain crises will be favoured and others ignored, much as the continuing tragedy in Afghanistan has largely been ignored in the West in the post-Cold War period. There is clearly a need for a more systematic form of situation assessment. There is also a need for the media covering humanitarian disasters to encourage more thoughtful and judicious discussion of possible responses, rather than simply implying, as they sometimes do, that external military intervention is the main mode of response and is relatively unproblematic.

Within many parts of the UN system there are means of gathering information and issuing warnings about impending disasters. Leading figures in such UN bodies as UNHCR and DHA, and also in non-UN bodies such as ICRC, can point to the stream of reports, press releases and memoranda they have issued, and which have not been followed by action. Partly this may be the problem of 'clutter', which is familiar to students of intelligence agencies. There are so many warnings of so many impending crises that it is hard for governments or UN bodies to know which ones really matter. As Gareth Evans has noted:

> While there is little doubt that it is important for the UN to have good sources of information about the whole range of emerging threats, disputes, conflicts and other security crises, the problem is not only the lack of information, but also the system's ability to absorb the enormous amount of incoming information, analyse and apply it in a meaningful way.[10]

77

The problem of early warning is sometimes in reality a problem of will and capacity. Information is received but not acted upon. Governments and international bodies can suffer from 'compassion fatigue' every bit as much as individuals; and also from the all-too-human tendency to put off problems till tomorrow. They may only be stirred from inactivity by the actual advent of disaster, or by powerful media campaigns.

Not surprisingly, the idea that a particular body should be charged with amassing relevant information and issuing a formal warning of impending disaster has gained strength. To an extent, DHA has this function, which could be further extended in crisis areas.[11] There are practical snags in proposals for a system of formal early warning. Some countries would vehemently object to being named publicly as the location of incipient catastrophe, and many UN officials sympathise with this. If, for example, Algeria was declared to be on the brink of civil war, a huge diplomatic earthquake would follow, and any advantage would be minimal.

Some have suggested that ICRC, being impartial and independent, should have a role as an independent issuer of warnings. The political constraints on making public pronouncements have decreased with the passing of the Cold War, but they have not disappeared. ICRC is reluctant to go beyond its current range of carefully modulated whistle-blowing. When ICRC issues a warning, it is to help the victims; on occasion, though, it may think twice, and act only confidentially.

The increasing recognition of the importance of early warning and prevention has led to a large number of new initiatives, one of which was the establishment in 1994–95 of the International Crisis Group (ICG), a private, non-profit corporation established partly on the basis of work at the Carnegie Endowment for International Peace in Washington DC. ICG aims to alert governments and the world community when it believes the time is right for mediation or other diplomatic efforts to avert incipient disasters and their huge human-itarian ramifications. As its prospectus says, 'ICG will set out to demonstrate that timely expenditure on preventive measures is not simply a moral necessity, but also an economic one'.[12]

An early warning system is only relevant if there is also an early action system. Yet in the experience of humanitarian organisations, early action is triggered not only by humanitarian concern, but by political pressure and by state interests. The central problem remains the world's will and capacity to respond.

CONCLUSIONS

The major increase in international humanitarian action in wars and other crises is the result not only of the end of the Cold War, but also of factors that have emerged over a long period and are likely to endure into the next century – the prevalence of civil wars and failed states, the anxiety of many countries to forestall refugee influxes by supporting humanitarian action in or near the country of origin, and the desire of the relatively secure (especially in Western democratic states) to do something about widely reported disasters. Frequently, when populations are threatened with starvation, eviction and death, it is impossible for outside bodies to do nothing. Not to act when there is the capacity to do so is itself likely to be a source of future recrimination and hostility. Even if humanitarian action goes through cycles of decline it will not disappear; it reflects interests as well as altruism. Decision-makers need to plan for such action, offer assistance, and be aware of its merits and weaknesses.

Humanitarian efforts have achieved some important results since 1991, especially in saving lives. It enabled Kurds stranded in the mountains in 1991 to return home to relative, albeit temporary, safety. It averted the worst consequences of famine in Somalia in 1992–93. It subsequently prevented or mitigated at least two widely predicted disasters – mass starvation in Sarajevo in the three winters starting in 1992–93, and the uncontrolled spread of the extensive outbreaks of cholera and dysentery in the camps on the borders of Rwanda in 1994.

Yet the overall record of humanitarian action in the wars of the 1990s has been flawed. An underlying problem has been the inability to ensure security. The lack of protection for aid convoys and activities has contributed, in some cases, to the war economy. The lack of protection for vulnerable populations, including in supposedly protected areas from Srebrenica to Sulaimaniya, has been shameful. This has caused dis-illusion and a feeling that in some instances such endeavours may actually prolong wars. What lessons are to be learnt from these failures?

An attempt must be made both to build on the substantial achievements of the humanitarian efforts of the post-Cold War era and to overcome the no less substantial failures. It is now widely agreed that such an attempt must involve a far higher level of accountability of organisations involved in such efforts; there has not been nearly enough clear, complete, truthful and timely reporting of what has and has not been achieved. Such an attempt requires a capacity to think in both strategic and humanitarian terms simultaneously, and to temper idealism with some tough realism about what net benefits can actually be achieved. In responding to the wars and crises of the present era, there are no tried and tested answers.

An exploration of the failures of humanitarian action in the security field has to begin by recognising a harsh truth. The adoption by states and international bodies of the banner of humanitarian action was associated with a policy vacuum, former Yugoslavia and Rwanda being the prime examples. The existence of such vacuums is not surprising. Faced with complex conflicts on which they have different perspectives and limited interests, individual states and international organisations will continue to find it easier to agree on humanitarian action than on definite political prescriptions. The unavoidable inhibitions against outside powers deciding the outcome of a local or civil war reinforces the likelihood of ending up with policies that are even-handed and bland. Humanitarian action may continue, sadly, to be a substitute for long-term policies and difficult strategic decisions.

Four critical questions are raised by the vastly increased international diplomatic and military involvement in humanitarian action. Can it be made more effective through more coordination? When humanitarian priorities are in conflict with each other, or with important policy considerations, what is to be done? Does humanitarian action, by its nature, have to be neutral, impartial and independent, or can it be associated with the use of armed forces, and support for a particular side in a conflict? Can the poor performance regarding the protection of aid activities and vulnerable populations be remedied in any way?

Effectiveness Through Coordination?
There has long been a school of thought that a major cause of the troubles faced by charitable efforts has been a lack of coordination. The sheer number of organisations involved, their duplication of activities, their competition for attention, and their herd instinct to rush to the same crisis while ignoring others, all add to the persuasiveness of this diagnosis, and have resulted in calls for better coordination.

The practice so far of coordination, especially among different UN agencies, has yielded ambiguous results. The attempt by DHA to coordinate the activities of different agencies and outside bodies is gaining some support, and has reaped significant benefits, especially in countries where it has a strong and respected local representative. However, there are limits to what can be achieved. These result partly from the unique identity and mission of each agency, and the sensitivities of UN member-states. Some Group of 77 members are nervous about the potential power of the DHA to coordinate activities in particular countries. There is also a potential clash of priorities between the agencies associated with development on the one hand and humanitarian relief on the other. Above all, the DHA still lacks the financial strength, stable leadership and professional expertise of some other agencies.

The current emphasis on coordination could lead to illusions about what it could achieve. Some aspects of humanitarian work, such as ICRC's treaty-defined roles, may be best done independently. Furthermore, if the main coordinating body is a UN one, its actions may be considered tainted by some belligerents because of the UN's other simultaneous activities. Moreover, the main problems facing these efforts are not lack of coordination, but a lack of resources, a lack of political will to act and a lack of convincing answers to the security dilemmas of conducting humanitarian action in situations of war and conflict.

Above all, the call for coordination is of limited relevance if the scope for humanitarian action is restricted, as it necessarily is in some situations. Professionals in humanitarian organisations are acutely aware of the limits of what such action can achieve. Many of them subscribe fully to the view that it is not a substitute for political, diplomatic and military actions needed to address and end conflicts. The primary preoccupation of the UN and many national governments with humanitarian action can easily seem to be a betrayal of their larger responsibilities, and leads some people involved to view such action critically, even dismissively.

Tension Between Humanitarian Priorities
One objective problem that has contributed to coordination difficulties is the tension that often exists between different humanitarian priorities, as well as between them and other policies. All good things do not come together. The implementation of international humanitarian law, or of human-rights law, may require action to be taken against one side, jeopardising the impartial distribution of relief. Similarly, if a peace agreement is reached at the end of a long war, those implementing its terms often have to choose between the key requirement of maintaining peace (which may involve, most basically, monitoring cease-fire lines between belligerents) and the further requirement of implementing the

more detailed provisions of a peace accord on such matters as conducting elections, cooperation in joint institutions, and the arrest of individuals for violations of the peace agreement itself or of general international humanitarian norms. Such dilemmas were faced by UN forces in Cambodia in 1992–93, and IFOR in Bosnia in 1995–96. Often in such cases, for better or for worse, outside forces put the fundamental requirement of maintaining the cease-fire first, and other considerations (including humanitarian ones) second.

The hideous issue of enforced population movements and so-called 'ethnic cleansing' exposes a brutally clear clash between humanitarian and hard-nosed realist approaches to managing conflict. No humanitarian approach can accept that populations can be terrorised out of their homes by nationalist zealots and never afforded the chance to return. Peace negotiations in the Arab–Israeli conflict, Cyprus, Bosnia and elsewhere have involved persuasive demands that a right to return should be accepted and implemented. Yet a lesson of many conflicts with an ethnic dimension is that where two peoples are divided by extreme mutual fears, they may need to remain apart, even in separate states, long enough to let the bitterness subside. UNHCR has reluctantly assisted in some population movements whose effects it deplores. In a world in which humanitarian norms are widely supported but *realpolitik* has not lost its power, there is a large gap between words and actions. The Dayton Agreement proclaims a right to return home, but IFOR assigns that a low priority because it can do so little to stop continuing terror against minorities.

The lesson of such difficulties is that the pursuit of humanitarian objectives itself requires the continuous exercise of judgement. Yet judgement in political decision-making is not facilitated by the circumstances in which it currently takes place – the Cable News Network (CNN) factor leading to pressure for action, the tendency of politicians to talk in soundbites, the pressure to think short-term rather than long-term, and the need to resort to the lowest-common-denominator language of multilateralism.

Impartiality and the Ethos of Humanitarian Work

Fuller recognition of the central importance of security to humanitarian action has serious consequences for some of the most cherished ideas underlying humanitarian work. The concepts of impartiality and neutrality, widely seen as key requirements of humanitarian action in war, need to be critically re-examined. Many humanitarian workers adhere to these ideas, not because they are unaware of their defects, but because the alternatives appear worse. ICRC, for example, is right to assert that vital services, such as visiting detainees, could not be carried out at all if the organisation was perceived as *parti-pris* in a conflict. Clearly for ICRC, as for most UN peacekeeping forces, impartiality is a priceless asset which is not to be lightly compromised or quickly abandoned.

However, some humanitarian organisations and activities are associated more with one side than another anyway. National Red Cross societies are often very close to their own political authorities, sometimes notoriously so, yet they may carry out useful actions within their own sphere. Completely independent aid agencies often develop sympathy for one side in a conflict, and may act as a means of raising international support for it. Moreover, in many conflicts in the 1990s humanitarian aid has not been seen as impartial by those whose opinions count, namely the belligerents. This (as well as the perception that outside powers are not serious about backing up their words with action) helps to explain why parties to conflicts have often blocked and even attacked humanitarian operations.

If impartiality has value, as it undoubtedly does, it also has defects. It may be hard to square with other policies being pursued simultaneously. If sanctions are imposed on a state because of its violations of humanitarian law, then the impartial distribution of aid to inhabitants of that state risks becoming a bad joke. If the UN Security Council or a regional alliance were to conclude that the best way to end a war is to give material support to one side, that may again involve in practice denying help to that side's adversaries, and even going so far as to turn a blind eye to certain violations of humanitarian norms by the side being assisted or its co-belligerents. If one side consistently violates a cease-fire agreement or refuses to accept an election result as part of a peace agreement, then to continue with certain aid programmes in its territory in the name of impartiality and neutrality may be a mistake.

The result of these pressures is that in actual practice the concept of impartiality often bursts at the seams. Still notionally supported, as with the arms embargo on all parties to the wars in former Yugoslavia, it may be covertly flouted in undercover diplomacy, secret arms shipments, and other activities of diplomats, armed forces and intelligence agencies.

The principle of impartiality, as a basis for humanitarian action in war, cannot and should not be abandoned, especially by those organisations whose daily work requires the cooperation of all belligerents. The reiteration of the principle in the Red Cross movement's 1994 Code of Conduct for relief workers is understandable. However, the Code's avoidance of all difficult issues, including security, renders it of limited value, and its endorsement by over 140 governments only confirms the impression that they do not always take humanitarian issues seriously. Similar problems arose with the December 1995 Madrid Declaration of representatives of prominent humanitarian agencies. In fact, many in such bodies as ICRC and UNHCR who have to work at the sharp end, being well aware of the limits of impartiality, do not advocate it as a general policy for states and intergovernmental organisations, which should properly view it as one starting point, not as a policy strait-jacket. With respect to many conflicts, fairness in exercising judgement (including humanitarian action) may be a better guide to policy than impartiality, and may point in different directions.

Security as a Key Aspect of Humanitarian Action
If the practice of the 1990s has proved anything it is that humanitarian assistance cannot realistically be considered in isolation from security issues. The cost of failing to address the protection issue is high, not just for those being assisted, and not just for humanitarian agencies and NGOs, but also for outside powers. The pattern of half-hearted guarantees and post-disaster evasions has reflected badly on the credibility of the UN Security Council, and also on that of major states for whom a reputation for dependability is an important asset.

The argument that no humanitarian effort can afford to be associated with particular external powers or uses of force does not stand up. The armed forces of individual countries, as well as those under UN auspices, have frequently been involved in humanitarian action. Some specialist technical tasks often have to be entrusted to armed forces, for example, dropping emergency food supplies to some besieged communities and de-mining. Some basic security and logistical tasks may be best performed by external military forces, as happened in the camps on Rwanda's borders in 1994.

There are several circumstances in which humanitarian action may need to be associated with threats and uses of force. The most obvious is when those being assisted need security above all else. Unless they can be rescued and taken far from the scene of the conflict, their security can seldom be ensured by neutral and impartial non-military action alone, least of all in bitter civil wars. If safety zones are to be proclaimed, there will normally have to be a will and capacity to deter attacks on them and to defend them. Force in some form may also be needed to maintain discipline among those being assisted, for example when a refugee camp contains armed bands, or when rioters threaten aid depots.

Implementating the laws of war – international humanitarian law – can also be an important aspect of protection, and can require some uses of force. To stop genocide, to prevent the slaughter of innocent civilians in a 'safe area', to ensure observance of rules about delivering aid, and to arrest those charged with war crimes may at times require a degree of coercive power and a willingness to get involved in a conflict. ICRC has repeatedly recognised that it is states that have the primary responsibility for ensuring implementation of the Geneva Conventions. A corollary is that states may sometimes have to use force in implementing them. In the nature of things they will do so with mixed motives, multiple purposes and questionable co-belligerents. NATO's *Operation Deliberate Force*, starting in August 1995 following Bosnian Serb atrocities at Srebrenica and Sarajevo, is a case in point. An incidental consequence of this reasonably tough line against the Bosnian Serb forces was that the performance of the humanitarian supply operation improved substantially in subsequent weeks.

Action by states to prevent atrocities and random killing can take other forms. If the international community's countless expressions of concern about the human disasters of contemporary wars are to mean anything the issue of anti-personnel land-mines, which are killing about 200 people a week, must be tackled more effectively. The contemporary uses, and indeed fundamental characteristics, of these weapons violate basic principles of the laws of war. A universal prohibition of their manufacture, sale and use will be hard to achieve, not least because some states are reluctant to agree to it. However, a prohibition, even if incompletely supported, could help limit the huge and pointless carnage they cause.

The revival of the idea of humanitarian intervention – of multilateral military involvements which do not have the consent of the country concerned – has represented a major means of linking humanitarian action and the use of force. While important results have been achieved, the varied experiences of northern Iraq, Somalia, former Yugoslavia, Rwanda and Haiti suggest that this approach may be flawed in practice, as well as much contested in theory. There have been certain important new elements, especially authorisation from the UN Security Council. However, there is no general agreement in the international community on the legitimacy of humanitarian intervention, still less on any agreed definition of the circumstances in which it might be justified. The recent cases confirm that powers are reluctant to take part in interventions where the costs are high, which of course includes situations of major ongoing war. Even when countries are willing to act, there is often a lack of clarity about commitments and goals. There is room for doubt as to whether 'humanitarian intervention' is an appropriate generic term to describe all aspects of such actions. The principle of non-intervention retains its importance, and only in the most exceptional cases is the international community likely to tolerate 'humanitarian intervention'. The UN-based interventionism of recent years seems to be ebbing.

The varied experience of attempts to protect vulnerable populations in war points to a central contradiction. On the one hand, it is clearly an illusion to suppose that force and humanitarianism exist in two separate and entirely distinct spheres. Protection is properly seen not as an occasional add-on to humanitarian relief supplies, but as a key aspect of the international community's response to wars and crises. On the other hand, in most conflicts it is far from obvious what kind of protection can be offered, and who is to provide it.

The difficulty of providing protection for vulnerable groups in the midst of ongoing conflicts is huge. Outside powers, whether under UN, NATO or any other auspices, may lack the political will to deploy forces on the spot and keep them there. Hence the tendencies of the Western powers to rely on air-power, with all its limitations, to protect safety zones, as in northern Iraq and the Bosnian 'safe areas', and to commit ground forces only for a limited period, as in Somalia. These tendencies are unlikely to change suddenly.

This explains why the answer to the question of what kind of protection is provided, and by whom, has frequently been UN peacekeeping. In some circumstances, for example post-war reconstruction, this can work effectively. However, experiments in the 1990s with deploying UN peacekeepers in situations of ongoing conflict to assist humanitarian relief efforts have not on the whole been successful: in Somalia, Rwanda and Bosnia such deployments repeatedly led to demands for new forces to be introduced with tougher mandates, and not under UN control. In each case this was done, albeit only temporarily. The evidence appears to be that multilateral peacekeeping forces under UN command and attached to the idea of impartiality are not normally able to act with the degree of commitment and decisiveness that the fast-changing and bloody situations of contemporary wars require.

The question of securing protection for vulnerable populations in their own countries – whether through the actions of states or of UN forces – cannot be permanently separated from the larger question of defining a policy in relation to ongoing conflicts. Security has to come from a local balance, and sometimes local parties and armed forces, with all their faults, may represent the best means of achieving a settlement.

The most promising approach to the role of the military in relation to humanitarian efforts is likely to be a pragmatic one. While not denying a role for UN peacekeeping forces, or for full-scale 'humanitarian intervention' in cases of extreme emergency, such an approach also stresses the importance of other forms of military protection and assistance, not all of which will necessarily be mandated by the UN Security Council or run under UN control. Local forces, host-country governments, outside powers, regional organisations and alliances may all have a role in providing such help. Sometimes the fact that the forces involved are those of a major power, which is not likely to tolerate their humiliation, may assist this role and have a deterrent function. Sometimes, too, a local power with a real interest in the outcome, and the determination to stay for as long as it takes, may achieve more results than a disinterested distant state whose public, or government, has a short attention span.

Above all, future attempts to protect populations in areas of conflict need to avoid the elements of ambiguity, verging on dishonesty, that have characterised many such efforts in the post-Cold War period. Such protection, for example through 'safety zones', requires clarity about the nature of the zones and the question of the legitimacy of military activity in them; it also requires major and sometimes long-term military commitments. It should only be extended when there is serious political support.

There are obvious risks in approaches that emphasise military support as a natural corollary of humanitarian action. The military could too easily see themselves as God's gift to humanitarian workers, whose proper concern with impartiality and independence make them prickly customers. A general perception that humanitarian action was but a harbinger of military involvement would exacerbate concern in target countries, and could be deeply damaging to humanitarian organisations. Further, there is always the possibility that what starts as military protection of humanitarian action may end as direct, unintended and unconstructive military involvement in a distant conflict. These risks are bound to lead to parsimony in the use of force, but should not deter states from providing military support for humanitarian purposes where it is genuinely needed, properly thought out, and has a prospect of achieving worthwhile results. The bland statements, half-promises and betrayals of the 1990s cannot be repeated without doing great harm, not just to those in need of assistance, but also to those states and organisations that seek to help them.

NOTES

Chapter I

[1] *Global Humanitarian Emergencies, 1995* (New York: US Mission to the UN, January 1995), p. 1. A subsequent edition of this report was published in February 1996.

[2] UN High Commissioner for Refugees (UNHCR), *The State of the World's Refugees 1995* (Oxford: Oxford University Press, 1995), pp. 19–20, 36, 248 and 255. The 1995 figure was supplied directly by UNHCR. See also the note of scholarly caution about the problem of refugee statistics, pp. 244–46.

[3] *Ibid.*, p. 247.

[4] Gil Loescher, *Refugee Movements and International Security*, Adelphi Paper 268 (London: Brassey's for the IISS, 1992), p. 5.

[5] *Ibid.*, p. 68.

[6] Yves Sandoz, 'Internally Displaced Persons', paper presented at UNHCR Subcommittee on International Protection, Geneva 18 May 1994.

[7] The expanded function was frankly recognised in a UNHCR document, 'Protection Aspects of UNHCR Activities on Behalf of Internally Displaced Persons', EC/1994/SCP/CRP.2, 4 May 1994. See also the useful discussion in *The State of the World's Refugees 1995*, pp. 19–55.

[8] Larry Minear and Thomas G. Weiss, *Mercy Under Fire: War and the Global Humanitarian Community* (Boulder, CO: Westview, 1995), pp. 21–22.

[9] Ali Mazrui, address at the Regional Institute of the League of Red Cross Societies, Dar-es-Salaam, 23 November 1970, quoted in David P. Forsythe, *Humanitarian Politics: The International Committee of the Red Cross* (Baltimore, MD: The Johns Hopkins University Press, 1977), p. 241.

[10] *Global Humanitarian Emergencies, 1995*, pp. 35–36, supplemented from the 1996 edition, and from other sources. Some of these expenditures are not war-related. In several cases the figure in the right-hand column is only that part of the agency's overall budget that is classified as related to humanitarian relief, emergency assistance, etc.

[11] *Ibid.*, 1996 edition, p. 22. Also, *Development Cooperation: Efforts and Policies of the Members of the Development Assistance Committee, Report 1995* (Paris: Organisation for Economic Cooperation and Development [OECD], 1996), p. 95.

[12] All Oxfam budget figures supplied directly by Ed Cairns of Oxfam, August 1996.

Chapter II

[1] US surveys reflecting the preoccupation with this theme have included Lori Fisler Damrosch (ed.), *Enforcing Restraint: Collective Intervention in Internal Conflicts* (New York: Council on Foreign Relations Press, 1993). This book was written when enthusiasm for collective intervention was widespread. Despite its title and optimistic theme, its analysis of particular cases is sober. For latter-day attempts at a more transformational view see Gene M. Lyons and Michael Mastanduno (eds), *Beyond Westphalia? State Sovereignty and International Intervention* (Baltimore, MD: The Johns Hopkins University Press, 1995).

[2] See Ian Forbes and Mark Hoffman (eds), *Political Theory, International Relations and the Ethics of Intervention* (London: Macmillan, 1993), and James Mayall (ed.), *The New Interventionism 1991– 1994: United Nations Experience in Cambodia, Former Yugoslavia and Somalia* (Cambridge: Cambridge University Press, 1996).

[3] For a succinct and sceptical survey of the history of 'humanitarian intervention' in international legal debate over the centuries, see Ian Brownlie, *International Law and the Use of Force by States* (Oxford: Clarendon Press, 1963), pp. 338–42.

[4] 'Humanitarian intervention' is viewed in both these senses in John Harriss (ed.), *The Politics of Humanitarian Intervention* (London: Pinter for the Save the Children Fund, 1995), pp. xi, 2–3, 8–9, etc.

[5] 'United Nations Interventions in Conflict Situations', a submission from Community Aid Abroad Australia, and Oxfam UK and Ireland, to Ambassador Richard Butler, Chair of the UN Preparatory Committee for the Fiftieth Anniversary (Oxford: Oxfam, February 1994), p. 10.

[6] 'Conclusion', in Hedley Bull (ed.), *Intervention in World Politics* (Oxford: Oxford University Press, 1984), p. 195. See also his remarks on p. 193 about the impact of 'the growing legal and moral recognition of human rights on a world-wide scale' on the question of humanitarian intervention.

[7] United Nations Security Council Resolution (UNSCR) 743, 21 February 1992, establishing UNPROFOR, not only specified that the Security Council was carrying out its responsibility 'for the maintenance of international peace and security' (i.e., it was acting under Chapter VII of the UN Charter), but also recalled the provisions of Article 25 (which requires UN member-states 'to accept and carry out the decisions of the Security Council in accordance with the present Charter').

[8] See UNSCR 758, 8 June 1992; UNSCR 761, 29 June 1992; and UNSCR 770, 13 August 1992.

[9] On the Rwanda catastrophe in 1994, and the humanitarian actions in relation to them, see especially *The International Response to Conflict and Genocide: Lessons from the Rwanda Experience* (Copenhagen: Steering Committee of the Joint Evaluation of Emergency Assistance to Rwanda, 5 vols., March 1996). For a critical account of the UN Security Council's role, see Study 2, *Early Warning and Conflict Management*, pp. 41–57. The discussion of security issues in this study is weak. The account of the response of the UN headquarters in New York to the crisis omits reference to some key documents. Further, there is no systematic exploration of what kind of military intervention might have protected the inhabitants, and how troops could have been found for it.

[10] For a critical view of the provisions and working of the 1948 Genocide Convention see Leo Kuper, *Genocide: Its Political Use in the Twentieth Century* (New Haven, CT: Yale University Press, 1982), pp. 36–39 and 174–85.

[11] Damrosch (ed.), *Enforcing Restraint*, p. 1.

[12] See the sceptical view on armed interventions for humanitarian purposes expressed by Yves Sandoz of the International Committee of the Red Cross (ICRC) in *International Review of the Red Cross*, no. 288, May–June 1992, p. 222.

[13] Gareth Evans, Australian Foreign

Minister at the time, enumerated a comprehensive list of conditions that would need to be satisfied in any case of intervention, and which were seen as a necessity if a 'right of humanitarian intervention' was to be recognised. Gareth Evans, *Cooperating for Peace: The Global Agenda for the 1990s and Beyond* (St Leonards, New South Wales: Allen & Unwin, 1993), p. 156.

Chapter III

[1] W. J. Bryan, US Secretary of State, to President Woodrow Wilson, 15 February 1915, in *Foreign Relations of the United States: The Lansing Papers 1914–1920* (Washington DC: US Government Printing Office [GPO], 1939), vol. I, p. 353.

[2] Bryan to Wilson, 18 February 1915, *ibid.*, p. 362. The (principally German) *quid pro quo* was to have been in three areas: certain limitations on the use of naval mines; submarines not to attack commercial vessels; belligerents not to use neutral flags on merchant vessels.

[3] Walter H. Page, US Ambassador to the UK, to the US Secretary of State, 27 February 1915. *Ibid.*, pp. 364–65.

[4] For documents on US involvement in relief operations in numerous countries in the latter stages of the First World War, see especially *Papers Relating to the Foreign Relations of the United States, 1918*, Supplement 2, *The World War* (Washington DC: GPO, 1933), pp. 459–647.

[5] David Bryer, 'Providing Humanitarian Assistance During Internal Conflicts', address to International Peace Academy Conference, Vienna, 23 July 1996, p. 3.

[6] Boutros Boutros-Ghali has said that safeguarding the concept and reality of 'humanitarian space' is 'one of the most significant challenges facing the humanitarian community'. *Confronting New Challenges: Annual Report on the Work of the Organization 1995* (New York: United Nations, 1995), p. 172. The concept was discussed with particular reference to Central America in Minear and Weiss, *Mercy Under Fire*, pp. 38–45.

[7] For an analysis which does not dwell on the possible conflicts between humanitarianism, human rights and peacekeeping, see the UN Joint Inspection Unit report by Francesco Mezzalama, 'Investigation of the Relationship Between Humanitarian Assistance and Peace-Keeping Operations', distributed to the General Assembly as UN document A/50/572, 24 October 1995.

[8] Statement by the President of the Security Council, UN document S/PRST/1994/22 of 3 May 1994, p. 2, discussing the Secretary-General's report, 'Improving the Capacity of the United Nations for Peace-keeping', UN document S/26450, 14 March 1994.

[9] *The Clinton Administration's Policy on Reforming Multilateral Peace Operations* (Washington DC: US Department of State Publication 10161, May 1994), 15 pp. This is virtually the text of Presidential Decision Directive 25, less some appendices. The two factors cited are both on p. 4.

[10] Figures supplied by UNHCR, Geneva, 12 February 1996.

[11] UNHCR, *The State of the World's Refugees 1995*, p. 126.

[12] The Berlin blockade lasted from 24 June 1948 to 12 May 1949. Figures for monthly tonnages delivered varied from 70,241 (June–July 1948) to 235,377 (April 1949), delivered by

14,036 and 26,025 sorties respectively. The airlift continued until September 1949, because of a railway strike and continued traffic restrictions, with even higher tonnages delivered. Robert Jackson, *The Berlin Airlift* (Wellingborough, Northants: Patrick Stephens, 1988), p. 146.

[13] 'Supplement to An Agenda for Peace: Position Paper of the Secretary-General on the Occasion of the Fiftieth Anniversary of the United Nations', UN document A/50/60, 3 January 1995, paragraph 34.

[14] *Ibid.*, paragraph 35.

[15] UNSCR 770, 13 August 1992. This point was reaffirmed in UNSCR 787, 16 November 1992.

[16] Photograph in *The Times*, 18 April 1991, p. 3.

[17] From remarks by Ogata at a conference on 'Conflict and Humanitarian Action', Princeton, NJ, 22–23 October 1993, quoted in Minear and Weiss, *Mercy Under Fire*, p. 21.

[18] 1949 Geneva Convention I, Article 23; and 1949 Geneva Convention IV, Article 14.

[19] 1949 Geneva Convention IV, Article 15.

[20] 1977 Geneva Protocol I, Article 60. See also Article 59, on 'Non-defended localities'.

[21] For a useful general survey, see Karin Landgren, 'Safety Zones and International Protection: A Dark Grey Area', *International Journal of Refugee Law*, vol. 7, no. 3, July 1995, pp. 436–58.

[22] The following is a selection of terms which have appeared in UN Security Council resolutions: 'security zone' (UNSCR 757, 30 May 1992, Sarajevo and its airport); 'United Nations protected areas (UNSCR 762, 30 June 1992, Croatia); 'safe area' (UNSCR 819, 16 April 1993, Srebrenica); 'neutral zone' (UNSCR 918, 17 May 1994, Kigali airport); and 'secure humanitarian areas' (UNSCR 925, 8 June 1994, Rwanda).

[23] The UNHCR stated in 1995 that there had not been a single death in an ORC in Sri Lanka as a result of military action. 'Safe Areas: A Substitute for Asylum?', *The State of the World's Refugees 1995*, p. 128. Between 1994 and mid-1996, thousands of people in the ORCs had returned home.

[24] Reports in *The Times*, 18 April 1991, pp. 1 and 3.

[25] UNSCR 819, 16 April 1993.

[26] UNSCR 824, 6 May 1993.

[27] UNSCR 836, 4 June 1993.

[28] See Gerald B. Helman and Steven R. Ratner, 'Saving Failed States', *Foreign Policy*, no. 89, Winter 1992–93, pp. 3–20; and Peter Lyon, 'The Rise and Fall and Possible Revival of International Trusteeship', *Journal of Commonwealth and Comparative Politics*, no. 31, March 1993, pp. 96–110.

[29] Explored further in Adam Roberts, 'The Laws of War: Problems of Implementation in Contemporary Conflicts', in European Commission, *Law in Humanitarian Crises*, vol. I, *How Can International Humanitarian Law be Made Effective in Armed Conflicts?* (Luxembourg: Office for Official Publications of the European Communities, 1995), pp. 13–82.

[30] ICRC special brochure, *Saving Lives: The ICRC's Mandate to Protect Civilians and Detainees in Bosnia-Herzegovina* (Geneva: ICRC, April 1995), pp. 3 and 9. This also gives impressive figures regarding ICRC visits to detainees (p. 13), and releases of detainees under ICRC auspices. The circumstances in which ICRC was prepared to make public

statements about violations had been outlined in 'Action by the International Committee of the Red Cross in the Event of Breaches of International Humanitarian Law', *International Review of the Red Cross*, no. 221, March–April 1981.
[31] For a useful survey of ICRC's role from 1945 to 1975, see Forsythe, *Humanitarian Politics*.
[32] UN Security Council Statement S/PV.2667, 21 March 1986.

Chapter IV
[1] From 'Fundamental Principles of the Red Cross', proclaimed by the XXth International Conference of the Red Cross, Vienna, 1965.
[2] 1977 Geneva Protocol I, Article 70.
[3] Points made with particular clarity by Nicholas Morris of UNHCR in a note on 'Humanitarian Aid and Neutrality', 16 February 1995.
[4] S. Neil MacFarlane, Larry Minear and Stephen D. Shenfield, *Armed Conflict in Georgia: A Case Study in Humanitarian Action and Peacekeeping* (Providence, RI: Thomas J. Watson Institute, 1996), occasional paper 21, p. x. This report was based on fieldwork in Georgia up to March 1995. Subsequently, and following the development of a more tolerant attitude on the part of the Georgian government, UNHCR and DHA have displayed greater sensitivity to humanitarian needs in their own right in Abkhazia and South Ossetia.
[5] 'Humanitarianism Unbound? Current Dilemmas Facing Multi-Mandate Relief Operations in Political Emergencies' (London: African Rights, Discussion Paper no. 5, November 1994), p. 2.
[6] *Ibid.*, p. 11.
[7] David Bryer, 'Lessons from Bosnia: The Role of NGOs', seminar paper at All Souls College, Oxford, 1 March 1996, pp. 2 and 5. See also the chapter 'A World at War' in *The Oxfam Poverty Report 1995* (Oxford: Oxfam, June 1996), pp. 42–70.
[8] David Bryer, letter to the author, 2 April 1996.
[9] International Federation of Red Cross and Red Crescent Societies, *World Disasters Report 1996* (Oxford: Oxford University Press, 1996), pp. 7 and 142.
[10] Cornelio Sommaruga, President of ICRC, at the UN General Assembly, 20 November 1992. *International Review of the Red Cross*, no. 292, January–February 1993, pp. 52 and 53.
[11] James C. Ingram, 'The Politics of Human Suffering', *The National Interest*, no. 33, Fall 1993, p. 60. Adapted from his chapter in Thomas G. Weiss and Larry Minear (eds), *Humanitarianism Across Borders* (Boulder, CO: Lynne Rienner, 1994).
[12] *The Lost Agenda: Human Rights and UN Field Operations* (New York: Human Rights Watch, 1993), p. 1. See also the similar arguments in *Peace-keeping and Human Rights* (London: Amnesty International, January 1994).
[13] 'Humanitarianism Unbound?', p. 4.
[14] *Ibid.*, pp. 4-5 and 11.
[15] Bryer, 'Providing Humanitarian Assistance During Internal Conflicts', p. 3.
[16] Personal communication from Nicholas Morris, UNHCR, 27 March 1995. See also the judicious discussion, 'Increased Emphasis on Human Rights', in *State of the World's Refugees 1995*, pp. 40–42.
[17] 'Humanitarianism Unbound?', p. 11.
[18] Described by a participant who later became Professor of International Relations, J.K. Zawodny, *Nothing But Honour: The Story of the Warsaw*

Uprising, 1944 (London: Macmillan, 1978), especially pp. 69–78.
[19] Cecil Woodham-Smith, *The Great Hunger: Ireland 1845–49* (London: Hamish Hamilton, 1962), especially pp. 410–11.
[20] 'Humanitarianism Unbound?', p. 7.
[21] Points 2, 4 and 9 of 'Code of Conduct for the International Red Cross and Red Crescent Movement and NGOs in Disaster Relief'. For more on this agreement, its background, and the NGOs subscribing to it, see *World Disasters Report 1996*, pp. 145–49. See also the general discussion of accountability, including a proposal for 'a new humanitarian watchdog', in Minear and Weiss, *Mercy Under Fire*, pp. 77–84 and 211.
[22] *The International Response to Conflict and Genocide*, Study 1, *Historical Perspective: Some Explanatory Factors*, p. 6; and Study 3, *Humanitarian Aid and Effects*, pp. 6 and 157.
[23] *The International Response to Conflict and Genocide – Synthesis Report*, p. 60.
[24] On Iraq's rejection of resources available to relieve suffering, see 'Situation of Human Rights in Iraq: Note by the Secretary-General', UN Document A/50/734, 8 November 1995, pp. 12–16.
[25] Quoted in Minear and Weiss, *Mercy Under Fire*, p. 69.
[26] Figures for emergency funding and overall ODA funding, and ample evidence of the concern of development assistance specialists about the rise in spending on emergency relief, can be found in *Development Cooperation Report 1994* (OECD), pp. 80–84; and *Development Cooperation Report 1995*, p.95. This concern is also noted in *World Disasters Report 1996*,

p. 62.
[27] R.M. Connaughton, *Military Support and Protection for Humanitarian Assistance: Rwanda April–December 1994* (Camberley, Surrey: Strategic and Combat Studies Institute, occasional paper no. 18, 1996), p. 4.
[28] For a sensitive exploration, highlighting elements of convergence between the attitudes of military and civilian groups, see Hugo Slim, 'The Stretcher and the Drum: Civil–Military Relations in Peace Support Operations', *International Peacekeeping*, vol. 3, no. 2, Summer 1996.
[29] Speech by Jan Eliasson in Atlanta, Georgia, 17 February 1993. Cited in Erskine Childers and Brian Urquhart, *Renewing the United Nations System* (Uppsala: Dag Hammarskjöld Foundation, 1994), p. 118.
[30] *Ibid.*, pp. 118 and 204.
[31] Joint Inspection Unit report, *Investigation of the Relationship Between Humanitarian Assistance and Peace-Keeping Operations*, October 1995, pp. ix and 28.
[32] The actual work of the UN volunteers in conflict and post-conflict situations is well described by participants in *Volunteers Against Conflict* (Tokyo: United Nations University Press, 1996).
[33] See UN General Assembly Resolution (UNGAR) A/49/139, 20 December 1994, and UNGAR 50/19 of 28 November 1995, both entitled 'Participation of Volunteers, "White Helmets", in Activities of the United Nations in the Field of Humanitarian Relief, Rehabilitation and Technical Cooperation for Development'.
[34] Quoted in Connaughton, *Military Support*, p. 18.
[35] *The International Response to Conflict and Genocide*, Study 3,

Humanitarian Aid and Effects, pp. 11 and 156–66. The volume entitled *Synthesis Report*, in discussing the protection of victims and the role of military contingents (pp. 48–49, 56 and 60), advocates that UN peacekeeping forces be given a clear mandate to protect civilians when large numbers are threatened by violence, but does not discuss the implications for the impartiality of UN forces.

[36] For example, 1907 Hague Convention IV, Regulations, Articles 21, 23 and 27; 1949 Geneva Convention IV, Articles 11 and 14–26; 1977 Geneva Protocol I, Articles 8–31, 37(1)(d), 38, 61–71 and 79.

[37] Boutros Boutros-Ghali, *Confronting New Challenges*, p. 229.

[38] For earlier discussions, see the 1971 Zagreb Resolution of the Institute of International Law on 'Conditions of Application of Humanitarian Rules of Armed Conflict to Hostilities in which United Nations Forces May Be Engaged', reprinted in Adam Roberts and Richard Guelff (eds), *Documents on the Laws of War* (Oxford: Oxford University Press, 2nd edition, 1989), pp. 371–75.

[39] UNSCR 758, 8 June 1992. Similar demands for the safety of UN and humanitarian personnel can be found in many subsequent resolutions on former Yugoslavia, including UNSCR 761, 29 June 1992; UNSCR 764, 13 July 1992; UNSCR 770, 13 August 1992; and UNSCR 802, 25 January 1993.

[40] UNSCR 925, 8 June 1994.

[41] Convention on the Safety of United Nations and Associated Personnel, approved by UNGAR 49/59, 9 December 1994, Article 1. Full text in UN document A/RES/49/59, 17 February 1995.

[42] Article 2(2), on scope of application, says: 'This Convention shall not apply to a United Nations operation authorised by the Security Council as an enforcement action under Chapter VII of the Charter of the United Nations in which any of the personnel are engaged as combatants against organised armed forces and to which the law of international armed conflict applies.'

[43] These figures, based on UN and US official sources, are mainly from ICRC, *Anti-personnel Landmines: Friend or Foe? – A Study of the Military Use and Effectiveness of Anti-personnel Mines* (Geneva: ICRC, March 1996), p. 9.

[44] See UNGAR 50/70 (O), and UNGAR 50/74, both adopted without a vote on 12 December 1995.

[45] ICRC, *Anti-personnel Landmines: Friend or Foe?*, pp. 71–73.

[46] Amended Protocol II to the 1981 UN Convention on Specific Conventional Weapons, Articles 1(2) and 3–12.

Chapter V

[1] David Bryer, 'Lessons from Bosnia: The Role of NGOs', p. 8.

[2] *The International Response to Conflict and Genocide*, Study 3, *Humanitarian Aid and Effects*, pp. 10, 122–36. On the coordination lessons, see also the *Synthesis Report*, pp. 57–59.

[3] Evans, *Cooperating for Peace*, pp. 158–59.

[4] DHA was established following UNGAR 46/182, 19 December 1991. For a survey of UN coordination efforts under the DHA, including details of the Central Emergency Revolving Fund, see 'Strengthening of the Coordination of Emergency Humanitarian Assistance of the United Nations: Report of the Secretary-General', UN document A/

49/177/Add.1, 1 November 1994.
[5] For figures on the actual income received by the UN Consolidated Inter-Agency Humanitarian Assistance Appeals, 1992–95, see Boutros-Ghali, *Confronting New Challenges*, p. 174.
[6] Toby Lanzer, *The UN Department of Humanitarian Affairs in Angola: A Model for the Coordination of Humanitarian Assistance?* (Uppsala: Nordiska Afrikainstitutet, Studies on Emergencies and Disaster Relief, no. 5), pp. 8, 10.
[7] 'United Nations Interventions in Conflict Situations', submission from Community Aid Abroad Australia, and Oxfam UK and Ireland, p. 14.
[8] This post was also established on the basis of UNGAR 46/182. For a brief account, see Tom J. Farer and Felice Gaer, 'The UN and Human Rights: At the End of the Beginning', in Roberts and Kingsbury (eds), *United Nations, Divided World* (Oxford: Oxford University Press, 2nd edition, 1993), p. 256.
[9] Early warning is discussed as a sub-category of preventive diplomacy in Boutros Boutros-Ghali, *An Agenda for Peace* (New York: United Nations June 1992), paragraphs 26 and 27.
[10] Evans, *Cooperating for Peace*, p. 70.
[11] In a country where emergency operations have commenced, an 'integrated early warning cell should be established within the DHA field coordination office'. Conclusion 6 of *The International Response to Conflict and Genocide*, Study 3, *Humanitarian Aid and Effects*, p. 158.
[12] International Crisis Group, 'General Prospectus' (London: October 1995), p. 2.